LANCASHIRE HALLS

MARGARET G. CHAPMAN

FRANK GRAHAM
6 Queen's Terrace, Newcastle upon Tyne, 2

Published 1971

SBN 900409 77 0

Printed in Great Britain by Fletcher & Son Ltd, Norwich
Bound by Richard Clay (The Chaucer Press) Ltd, Bungay, Suffolk

GEOGRAPHIA

To
My Mother and Father
who have dedicated their lives to me
and to
My brother George
who died 27th April, 1967
Their kindness I will remember always

MARGARET G. CHAPMAN

Born in Winton, Eccles, Manchester, after only one year at school arthritis forced me to leave, and most of my young life was spent in hospitals.

We removed to Houghton Lane, Swinton, Manchester, living there over thirty years. Fortunately surrounded by many friends, life was interesting. I bought some oil paints, and won many prizes in amateur art exhibitions.

In 1949, my first painting was hung in Salford City Art Gallery—a portrait of my brother George, who died in 1967.

Four years later, a small self-portrait in gouache was shown on television 'Woman's Hour' by Mervyn Levy.

In 1954 broke my left arm.

In 1955, on joining the Salford Art Club, at Chaseley Field Adult Centre, Salford, I learned a great deal from criticism, practical demonstrations and lectures from experienced painters. Also taking lessons from the Club Chairman, Eric Satchwell—an excellent teacher, then Art Master at Salford Grammar School, and now Chief Lecturer and Art Master at The James Graham Teacher's Training College, Leeds, who previously living nearby, helped me overcome many painting problems.

Three of my works were shown in the North-West Federation of Art Societies first exhibition, held at Lewis's Manchester. And a year later in 1958, won second prize in a national painting contest organized by Mervyn Levy, with a self-portrait chosen from four thousand entries, by judges Sir John Rothenstein and Professor Gilbert Spenser, who referred to the painting as a 'Remarkable Document'. This was afterwards hung in the Walker Galleries, London.

Further success came my way in 1959, when seven paintings were shown in a Local Artist's exhibition at the Public Hall, Pendlebury, held in connexion with the Borough's Charter celebrations.

In September of the following year I had the honour of staging the first 'one-artist' exhibition ever held in the same hall. The show was organized by Mr G. B. Cotton, then Borough Librarian of Swinton and Pendlebury, later Salford City Librarian, and now Senior Lecturer in Librarianship at the Manchester College of Commerce. This occasion was graced by the presence of Miss Violet Carson. Three of my paintings were bought by the Corporation, and one by His Worship the Mayor, for the Town. Out of a total of fifty pictures on display, seventeen were sold.

Two more 'one-artist' exhibitions followed in 1961. The first was held at Gibb's Bookshop, Manchester, and the second in Monks Hall Museum, Eccles. That same year I broke my leg and had difficulty in working with it completely encased in plaster, but once more pressed on regardless.

In 1962, came a further exhibition, in Salford City Art Gallery; this was also honoured by Miss Violet Carson who made a lovely speech on my behalf.

Later, another show at Warrington Art Gallery, and various smaller ones, were held. Both Salford Art Gallery and Monks Hall Museum have my paintings in their permanent collections.

In 1963, I received an 'Award of Merit' on the recommendation of the famous artist L. S. Lowry, R.A., in a national contest, for a painting entitled 'Deserted Cottage, Boothstown', which was exhibited at the Alpine (Club) Gallery, London, in South Audley Street. This painting lived up to its name as it vanished, possibly during the journey from London to Salford Gallery, where the show was later repeated, and has never turned up to this day.

Another painting, 'The Artist's Father' was hung in the Royal Society of Arts, London, in 1964, and shown on television.

The following year, in April, I removed with my parents to a bungalow in Allenby Road, St Annes, having previously joined the Manchester 'Scribbler's Club' for writers, although so far had only written a few short poems. Feeling unsettled I bought a typewriter feeling rather doubtful about being able to use it. But fortunately managed. After taking a postal course on short story writing for children from Arthur Waite, of Bridge Street, Manchester, I've had many published both for children and adults.

As a member of the Lytham St Annes Art Society I exhibit in the annual exhibitions. In 1967, held a 'One artist' show there. In the same year annual show, a painting of an outsize 'Kipper' which I named 'Larger Than Life' was bought by Lanigan's fish shop owner Mrs Dent. This was hung in the main shop. Mrs Dent showed a photograph of myself painting The Packet House, Worsley, to a friend, who recognizing it as his grandfather's old home wanted to buy the painting. No longer having this in my possession I painted another much larger one. Mr Hilton came from Worsley, and now lives at Lytham, I was also commissioned to paint his house there. Coming from an old Worsley family, his grandfather had been employed at Worsley Halls.

In 1969, had an exhibition at Manchester Central Library which was shown on B.B.C. Television by Stuart Hall in the 'Look North' programme. At this time I broke the other leg badly, so didn't see it. The crowning achievement was when Mr Frank Graham kindly accepted this book for publication.

My career has not been easy, there have been many obstacles to overcome, and I foresee a lot more in the future, but each achievement, however small, has more than made up for the effort put into it.

I trust that like my paintings, this book will bring to others some of the pleasure experienced in its creation, for this will prove that despite limitations, I've done something in life worth while.

There have been many months of research, but the owners of the Halls and those responsible for their care, as well as other important personages, have been exceedingly kind and some have disclosed information never before published. With this knowledge I trust the first edition of Lancashire Halls will be a success.

MARGARET G. CHAPMAN
1970

AGECROFT HALL

Although this stately home no longer graces our countryside, Agecroft Hall is worthy of mention. Presumed to have been built about the time of Richard II (1377-1399), this fine relic of Old England originally stood in Pendlebury, one of the Lancashire towns which inspired many of the wonderful paintings by the world famous northern artist Laurence Stephen Lowry, R.A., and was situated about three miles north-west of Manchester Cathedral, and one mile and a half south of Prestwich.

A half-timbered defensive building, forming a complete quadrangle, about 100 feet square on plan, and comprising of some fifty rooms, this Hall was at one time surrounded by a moat which later became a fish pond. Just below the centre window of the upper storey at the front of House a badge, thought to have been that of Richard II with a white hart couchant, formed part of what was believed to be the original structure. Entrance was through an arched gateway in front of edifice. Originally open galleries overlooking the courtyard extended round all four sides, but they were later enclosed, also the cloister beneath them.

The interior of the House was much altered and modernized yet still retained its character. The Library windows were decorated with the arms of the Langleys, and the principal one with those of John of Gaunt, Duke of Lancaster, which were said to have been presented to him by the Langleys. This room was at one time the private Chapel. Another window bears the red and white rose emblem of the union of the houses of York and Lancaster. The flower stems being entwined between the letters H.E. answering to the date 1485, which was the year Henry VII married Elizabeth, daughter of Edward IV thus uniting the two rival houses. A different version was that Agecroft Hall was built about that time, but this window could have been put in later. A long corridor extending the full length of the upper storey front had a window bearing the heraldic badge of Edmund de Langley, Duke of York.

Over the Drawing Room door, let into the wainscot were eight emblematical figures carved in bold relief representing 'war and peace' which once formed part of a pulpit in the private Chapel of the House. For a short time after the death of Mr Dauntes part of the Hall was occupied by a farmer, who turned the pulpit into a cupboard. However it was later decided to use it as a decorative feature. There was in this room a half-length portrait of William Dauntes Esq., dressed in court armour of Elizabeth Is reign, also a portrait of Sir Edward Chisenhall the Royalist Commander, with his wife, and daughter who later married Christopher Dauntesey Esq. (ob. 1711). Sir Edward took part in the siege of Lathom House, and served under Prince Rupert at Marston Moor being a Colonel of a Royalist Regiment.

The Hall was nearly demolished when it was proposed to run a line of railway between Manchester and Bolton. A Mr Buck spent about £5,000 in contesting the project, eventually achieving a slight diversion of route.

In 1926, Agecroft Hall was bought by Thomas C. Williams Jr of Richmond, U.S.A. And it was carefully dismantled—no easy task, the Great Hall rose over two storeys and had a Minstrel's Gallery, and a most magnificent mullioned bay window measuring 10 feet high and 25 feet long—this window was kept in one piece, and each stone and beam etc. was numbered and crated and transferred from surroundings of coal mines (tunnels had even been dug under the building and subsidence became a possible danger) to Richmond, Virginia, U.S.A. where it was rebuilt in a beautiful setting similar to that of its early days in England. Now standing in Sulgrave Road, amidst landscaped gardens and terraces overlooking the historic James River, the hall is open to the public in Richmond as a typical example of English Elizabethan 'magpie' architecture through the generosity of Mrs David C. Morton and her late husband Mr Thomas C. Williams Jr, and house and gardens are managed by the Agecroft Association.

We in Britain are the poorer for the loss of this fine interesting hall, (money is no substitute for a work of art), but our loss is another Country's gain, and we may feel a certain pride in knowing American people appreciate our ancestral homes so much and go to such great lengths to acquire and preserve part of our English History.

ASHTON HALL

ENTERING through an avenue of trees one is impressed with the mediaeval appearance of this hall with its castellations and towers, but apart from the Old Tower the house was actually built in the middle of the nineteenth century. In its beautiful setting amidst some fine old trees one can look across fresh green meadows and see the outline of the Pennine Chain (on the eastern side). On the west is the Lune Estuary which eventually reaches Morecambe Bay. While to the north you can see the Lakeland Hills and Fells in Cumberland and Westmorland.

Views of the hall before the date it was rebuilt show the main wing to have been two storeys above the lofty basement with the principal entrance on the west side facing what is known as the Green Court.

Dr Whitaker was of the opinion that the walls throughout the building not only those of the tower were of the age of Edward III. The Tower measures internally in the basement 50 feet 10 inches × 25 feet 10 inches, the greater length being from west to east, and is 42 feet in height to the top of the battlements from the present ground level, but this has been raised 5 feet. The walls are 6 foot thick constructed of rubble masonry with mixed sandstone and gritstone in large irregular blocks with gritstone quoins and ashler parapet.

Little but the shell of the tower now remains, the interior being wholly modernized and divided up and all the original features either destroyed or concealed. The history of the original hall was full of exciting incidents.

For seven generations Ashton Hall has been, or was in the possession of the Dukes of Hamilton until 1853, and in the same year, after the death of the tenth Duke, the estates were sold to various public bodies and private purchasers. Ashton Hall became the property of Nicholas de Gendre Starkie who built the hall adjoining the Old Tower.

Mr James Williamson, M.P., later Lord Ashton, bought the property in 1884. When he died in 1931, the Hall was bought by Mr W. M. Pye, from whom the Lancaster Golf Club secured the present Course on a long lease, a new Company having been formed for administrative purposes in 1932. Everything is beautifully organized and the new Club House has every comfort for Golfers. There is a tea room, and a smoke and billiard room, and a special club for the Ladies.

The Course was laid out by the late James Braid, and Ashton Hall is still surrounded by ladies and gentlemen who are proud indeed of their Golfer's Paradise now known as a Golf and Country Club.

ASTLEY HALL

IN a beautiful well-wooded park, adjacent to the shopping centre of Chorley, and within one mile from the Town Hall, stands Astley Hall, which many years ago was granted to the Military Order of St

AGECROFT HALL.

SOUTH-WEST DOOR
AGECROFT HALL.

ASHTON HALL.

John of Jerusalem, the tenants being the Charnocks of Charnock. It came into their possession subject to a small quit-rent.

During the reigns of John, and Henry III, Adam de Chernoc, the first Lord bearing the territorial name, appears to have been joint Lord of Astley with Henry de Lee, Kt, and was the progenitor of a long line of feudal Lords of Charnock, Astley, and many neighbouring lands. His descendant Robert Charnock, of Astley, was one of the defenders of Lathom House, and also fought in the Civil Wars. The last of the male line, he died in 1653, previously having compounded for his estate in 1646 for the sum of £200, and by the marriage of his daughter Margaret, the last heiress of the Charnocks, the estate passed to Richard Brooke, of Mere, in Cheshire.

Later, by the marriage of Susanna, the only daughter of Peter Brooke, with Thomas Townley Parker, of Cuerden, in 1787, the property passed to her son Robert Townley Parker, of Cuerden.

In 1883, Astley Hall was owned by Thomas Townley Parker. On the death of the second Thomas Townley Parker in 1906, Astley Hall passed to his nephew Reginald Arthur Tatton, whose beneficient gift made it the property of the Corporation of Chorley in 1922, and it was opened to the public in 1924, by Arnold Gillett, then Chairman of the Parks Committee.

Her Majesty's Office of Works has scheduled Astley Hall as a 'Monument' to be preserved in the national interest. So this stately building will remain in all its magnificence and with treasures for all to see.

This Elizabethan Mansion, the oldest part of which dates back to the sixteenth century, was originally half-timbered, with stone-slated roof. The front was reconstructed in 1666, and a wing added in 1820. At first the walls were brick with stone dressings, these were later coated in plaster. The Hall is built around three sides of a central courtyard. So during the seventeenth century the whole of the main front was rebuilt in the style of the Jacobean Period, and another storey added. This made the Hall much more imposing, and the view from the upper stone-mullioned windows is remarkable.

The front door leads into the Great Hall, which measures 30 feet by 26 feet and is the height of two storeys. The arms of the Charnocks and Brookes are above the fireplace, and there are also a series of fascinating wood panel portraits of about the seventeenth century. These include Sir Francis Drake, 1540-1596; Queen Elizabeth I, Henry IV of France, and one of William, Prince of Orange, 1650-1702, to name only a few. There are also many other paintings of the Brooke and Townley Parker families. Here can be seen an oak banqueting (or Refectory) table 17 feet 9 inches long with eight bulbous-turned legs, which was brought to Astley by Robert Townley Parker from Extwistle Hall, Nr. Burnley, which was formerly the seat of the Parker family. Also here is a long oak chest, with seven panels carved in foliate design bearing initials and date 'L.R.E., 1665', in centre panel— a fine piece of work.

A very grand oak staircase opposite the front door leads to the upper rooms.

The ceilings at Astley Hall are delightful but the one in the Drawing Room is truly magnificent surpassing them all. A massive wreath encloses an oval space where are set scallop shells and infants at play. This ceiling is so outstanding that it is impossible to describe such beauty, and is one of the most elaborate specimens of plasterer's art in the County. The delicate ceiling ornaments are constructed of lead which is made to imitate plaster of Paris. This was done by Manchester artist Mr C. J. Lea, who also decorated other parts of the House.

In the Inlaid, and Dining Rooms hang more family portraits. An outstanding one is that of Thomas Brooke, Sheriff of Cheshire, when aged thirty years. This is full-length, and incorporated with the panelling of inlaid work. (This part of the House was added in 1820.) There is a Portrait of a Lady, attributed to Sir G. Kneller. Another of Oliver Cromwell; Thomas Townley Parker who married Susanna Brooke, of Astley; Robert Townley Parker (aged 17); and Robert Charnock, of Charnock and Astley, and others. Some interesting furniture includes an oak chest and cabinet of Jacobean checkered design, inlaid with bone.

The Art Gallery is a wonderful top-lighted room, and has a permanent collection of paintings, pottery, and glass etc. Lancashire Artists are encouraged to exhibit their work here, where exhibitions of paintings and photography are held.

In the Long Gallery, which occupies the whole length of the front of the House, is a shovel-board table, the finest of its kind known to exist. It is $23\frac{1}{2}$ feet long and elaborately ornamented. No one could say it hasn't a leg to stand on, for it has twenty, and is of very solid construction. They were prepared for heavy meals in the day when that was built.

In one bed-chamber stands the Cromwell Bed. A mighty creation of English oak, with rich carvings of great beauty.

Other Rooms have their own special interests, and among treasures at Astley Hall is attractive Leeds Pottery, bequeathed to the Corporation of Chorley by the late Robert Grey Tatton, Esq., in 1934, and antique glass purchased by the Corporation.

Within this imposing building, which is warm and friendly inside with its central-heating, are many things of interest. We are indeed fortunate to have such an inheritance.

BARCROFT HALL

ON the outskirts of Towneley Park, about $2\frac{1}{2}$ miles east of Burnley, stands Barcroft Hall, which was built in 1614, by William and Susan Barcroft, on the site of an older house. William the Conqueror gave the land to an ancestor of William Barcroft for services rendered during the Conquest.

Barcroft Hall was originally built in the E-plan style, but various alterations have since been made to the rooms.

The Great Hall, which measures 36 feet long by 24 feet wide and 14 feet high has a ceiling composed of large moulded oak beams. An imposing Ingle Nook commands attention at the east end, originally adjoining a solid circular stone staircase which is now no longer complete. The massive stone structure of this hall from the outside is very impressive, and it has stood the test of time remarkably well over the centuries.

THE IDIOTS CURSE

Tradition says that one of the heirs of William Barcroft was an idiot, we would prefer to say today— mentally disturbed, and that his younger brother fastened him by a chain in one of the cellars, where he starved to death. The brother reported him dead

ASTLEY HALL.

long before he actually *was*, which was in 1641, and thus obtained possession of the property.

It is said that during one of his lucid moments the prisoner pronounced a curse on the Barcroft family to the effect that the name should perish for ever, and the property would pass into other hands. The curse was said to have been fulfilled in Thomas Barcroft who died in 1688 without a male heir. The property then passed to his daughter Elizabeth, who conveyed it in marriage to Henry Bradshaw of Marple Hall, Cheshire. Their daughter Mary Bradshaw, heiress, was married to William Pimlot, and they had a son John. Mary Pimlot married twice, her second husband being Nathaniel Isherwood of Bolton-le-Moors, whose grandson Thomas Bradshaw Isherwood, came into possession of the estate on the death of the last Pimlot. He died in 1791, unmarried, and in 1795 his executors sold the Hall to Charles Towneley, a celebrated antiquary.

For many years Barcroft Hall was used as a Dower House, and when the Towneley estate was later sold the land on which the Hall stands was bought by a local farming family who added an extension to the north end for use as farm cottages. So Barcroft Hall is serving a useful purpose.

BARLOW HALL

As I have elsewhere referred to the legends, folklore, and ghosts of the place, we can go a little farther afield to the *time-honoured* but *little* known hall of Barlow. Even with my life-long knowledge of Didsbury, its history, and its public life and records, it is somewhat of a puzzle to say which is or which has been Didsbury, and which is or was *Barlow*.

Strictly speaking, Barlow seems never to have been anything but a *hall* and a *moor*. It was neither parish nor township, and yet there are several records where mention is made of the lordship and the manor of Barlow. The Hall was the home of one eminent family for four-hundred years. An intensely conservative family; more than one of whose members sacrificed everything, even to life itself, for their faith.

It is a wonder that Barlow Hall has not vanished, but it is in a secluded, lonesome part of the old moor, and near to the river Mersey. It is now two or three hundred yards outside the boundary of Didsbury township, being included in Chorlton-Cum-Hardy. Just three-hundred years ago there were lawsuits about the manorial rights and encroachments on the waste grounds of the moors of Didisburye and Chollerton or Chowreton, the Barlows of Barlow Hall being complained of.

In 1397, a certificate from Lichfield, beginning 'In Dei Noie, Amen' (In the name of God, Amen), says that Thomas de Barlow is the sole lord of Barlow, there having apparently been the usual litigation. Skipping over a few more years let us notice that twice on the present house is the date 1574. On the dial on the wall is written 'Lumen me regit 1574 VOS UMBRA' (The light rules me, the shade rules you). There may be some reference here to the frequent changes of faith which were then common.

In what is sometimes called the Chapel Window, a fine old window which faces the east, there is the same date, the initials A.B. several shields of arms, the Earl of Derby's being one, and the mottoes 'PRIST EN FOYTE' and RESPICE FINEM. These mottoes appear to have been used as guides, constancy in faith to the end.

Shortly after rebuilding of the house, namely in 1584, it was searched for priests. None were found, but the master was dragged to prison in Manchester where he soon afterwards died, and was buried at Didsbury.

The registers record 'Alexander Barlowe de Barlow, esquyer'. His son Sir Alexander, in his will said 'YF YT fortune I die within twentye myles of my house of Barlowe, that my sayd bodye be leyde in Didisburye Church, as neere unto my father as may be,' but they buried him by torchlight at Manchester. This Sir Alexander was married at four years old, renounced that wife, and married the daughter of Sir Uryan Brereton, of Honford by whom he had fourteen children. His picture has often been engraved. One of his sons was Rudesind, the President of the English Benedictines, and a more famous one was Edward the Martyr. The Didsbury Church register still plainly shows the entry of baptism: 'Nov 30 1585, Edwarde the sonne of Alex Barlowe, gent.' The name he assumed when admitted a Benedictine was Ambrose. He seems to have been a devout ascetic, living on 'whitmeats and garden stuff', of mean apparel, averse to play or feasting, would not look at a woman, always minding his work and finally was taken by a minister, who some accounts say was the Vicar of Eccles, in his surplice, accompanied by men with clubs and swords, on Easter Day, 1641. He was taken to gaol at Lancaster where he confessed he was a priest, and sentence of death was soon passed.

When dragged on a hurdle to execution some 'ministers of religion' persisted in trying to 'convert' him. He endured to the end, was hanged and quartered, and boiled in tar.

I have seen his skull. It is in 'The house of the skull,' (See Wardley Hall chapter), another of our old halls. As to the ghosts of Barlow it is better to be silent.

'On Sundaye,' the 26th May 1644, that is less than three years from this tragedy, 'Prince Rupert and his army encamped on Barloe More' on their rush to succour Bolton and Lathom House, and it is most likely that the Prince and his officers would rest in Barlow Hall, for the Barlows would be sure to be on the King's side, though that shifty King had let their brother die. In 1620, all the family had acknowledged to be recusants and continued to baptise their children at Didsbury.

In the next century, when Prince Charles Edward came to Manchester in the famous '45' Lord Elcho and his cavalry went south by the Barlow ford, an old ford of the Mersey near to Barlow Hall. The main army built and crossed by the first bridge over the Mersey between Didsbury and Cheadle. The Barlows seem to have again got into trouble over the Stuart cause. In fact their troubles and persecutions thickened. In 1734, I find mention of a dispute about the 'consecrated goods or ornaments in the Popish Chapel at Barlow'. In 1785, at the Bull's Head in Manchester the manor of Lordship of Barlow, with the hall etc. was offered for sale at auction. Samuel Egerton of Tatton, who bought it, was the sole acting executor of the last Barlow of Barlow, a family who had held the estate for 500 years. Its recent rise in value, the unearned increment, should exceed the wildest dreams of avarice.

ABOVE Extracts from Pilgrimages to old homes, by Fletcher Moss.

Above: BARLOW HALL.
Below: BARCROFT HALL.
On right: BORWICK HALL.

BARLOW HALL (private) thirteenth century. Now known as Chorlton Golf House.

There is no more historical clubhouse in the county. Figured prominently in the turbulent days of the religious persecution in the fifteenth and sixteenth centuries.

An upper room off the courtyard which remains practically untouched was the Chapel from which Father Barlow was dragged from his bed and taken to his execution at Lancaster in—1641. Decorative improvement and the installation of electric lighting are the only major alterations made to the buildings. The ancient oak roof timbers remain in position. The ancient moat still exists.

Many Americans have cast longing eyes on the stained glass windows but they are the property of the Egertons of Tatton. Long may they remain so.

BERNSHAW TOWER

BERNSHAW TOWER was a small fortified building which at one time stood in a beautiful ravine branching off from the great gorge of Cliviger about five miles from Burnley, and not far from the Eagle's Crag.

The last owner, Lady Sybil, was renowned for her wealth, beauty, and intelligence. Her fascination for the Eagle's Crag was uncanny, and her longing to possess supernatural powers grew until she was said to have sold her soul to the devil in order that she might join the Lancashire Witches in their nightly revelries. Her longing for excitement knew no limits.

Hapton Tower, was owned by Lord William Towneley, who had long been one of Lady Sybil's suitors only to be rejected. Despondently he decided to consult the famous Lancashire witch Old Mother Helston, who with magic spells assured him of success on 'All Hallow's Eve'. On the *day*, following her instructions, he went hunting, and on approaching the Eagle's Crag, saw a milk-white doe. He searched the country for miles, returning exhausted to the crag. Mother Helston appeared in the disguise of a strange hound which was sent to capture Lady Sybil (the white doe). Lord William was almost thrown into a steep abyss, but as the doe made for a precipice the hound seized her by the throat, holding on until Lord William threw an enchanted silken leash round her neck, and took her home with him to Hapton Tower. That night a fearful earthquake shook the Tower and the following morning the captured doe appeared back as the heiress at Bernshaw. After counter-spells her powers of witchcraft were overcome, and Lord William married Lady Sybil and took her to his home. But within a year she'd returned to her witchcraft and one time appeared in Cliviger Mill in the form of a white cat, only to have a paw cut off by the man-servant Robin as he watched by the Miller. Lady Sybil was discovered next morning pale and exhausted, but when Robin arrived at the Tower carrying a Lady's hand the mystery was solved, and by some magical power the hand with diamond ring was restored to the arm leaving a red mark round the wrist. Her angry husband was long before he forgave her. After this the Lady's health failed and she grew weak. As her life drew to its close, with the help of the local clergy, the devil's bond was overcome and Lady Sybil died peacefully.

Bernshaw Tower remained empty ever after and tradition says she was buried near the Eagle Crag, and that on All Hallow's Eve the milk-white doe and hound appear on the crag and are chased by a ghostly huntsman.

BORWICK HALL

BEGINNING with a Pele tower in about 1540, Borwick Hall, Near Carnforth, gradually grew until 1595, into the stately Elizabethan Manor which we see to this day.

The earliest owner of the manor of Borwick was thought to have been Patrick de Berewick in 1228, a time when buildings were mostly made of wood, and from the thirteenth to fifteenth centuries people in the district lived in constant terror of marauding Scots as they advanced southward over Shap Fell, burning down the wooden homes of the Lords of Borwick while on their journey to Lancaster during the raid of 1322. After this the pele tower was built to give greater protection, and as the oldest part of Borwick Hall, formed an extremely strong dwelling place being specially built for defence, and the turrets at the top give a castle-like appearance.

Two distinct types of architecture are evident in the present hall. The north wing was the first addition made to the tower, this was built by the Redmayne family in 1542. Charles II is said to have slept in one of these rooms during his journey to the battle of Worcester, and his army was encamped on Bartleholme.

In 1567, Robert Bindloss, a wool and cloth merchant from Kendal, acquired Borwick Hall and it remained the property of the Bindloss family for three-hundred years. The east wing is presumed to have been added by Robert Bindloss shortly after he bought the House.

The long barns at the west side were built in 1590. Here weary packhorses used to rest before continuing on their way to London, while their riders slept above. The west wing which was completed in 1595, was also added by the first Robert Bindloss. This extends to the left of the main entrance and is considered to be the most important part of the House, and shows something of the Bindloss family wealth. The Great Staircase which was built at the same time, provided access to the upper rooms of the tower. The newel stairs in the tower were removed.

Alixander Brinsmead an architect, was responsible for the design and building of the west wing. On a stone slab supported by pillars at the top of the Great Staircase, his name is inscribed thus:

ALIXANDER BRINSMEAD, mason. 1595

The Gate House was built in 1650.

Many of these places claim to have a ghostly presence, but Borwick Hall is said to have *two*. First a fair young maiden who faded and died in the long attic where she was kept a prisoner for refusing to marry the man of her father's choice. Her unhappy spirit lingers weightless yet earthbound. And there is a cavity of about four feet deep beneath the floor boards of one of the first floor rooms said to have been a hiding hole for Catholic Priests. The story goes that Robert Bindloss the third; *Sir* Robert Bindloss, on discovering a Priest hiding there, slew him,

BROWSHOLME HALL.

Painting, Margaret Chapman.

and that the ghost of this priest sadly haunts the corridors.

Borwick Hall, with its lovely gardens, is the property of W. S. Haworth Esq., and is open to the public.

BROWSHOLME HALL

BROWSHOLME HALL, is actually in Yorkshire, less than a mile from the River Hodder, which forms the boundary between Yorkshire and Lancashire to the South. Although the Forest of Bolland was for some centuries the property of the Duchy of Lancaster, of the 66,000 acres, 6,000 only were in Lancashire. Well! 6,000 acres is quite a lot, and as this Hall is so intensely interesting I feel compelled to include it in this book.

Browsholme Hall, is the Historic Home of the Parker family; I repeat 'Home', because despite the splendour, it still remains a much-loved home in the true sense of the word.

The family surname was adopted in the fourteenth century (which was the time when surnames first came into use in Britain). Parker or Park-keeper being the office held by the son of Peter de Alancotes from whom Colonel Robert Parker, the present owner is directly descended.

The Parker had to be well-versed in reading, writing, accountancy, and the law. Many owners of Browsholme Hall have graduated at Cambridge, and held the distinctions of High Sheriff; Deputy Lieutenant, and Justice of the Peace.

The original House of timber and daub, was built by Richard Parker in 1507. Edmund Parker, built the present stone house.

The owner in 1604 was Thomas Parker, who purchased the Vaccary of Browsholme from the Crown, and employed the famous Elizabethan architect Thomas Holt of York, to re-front the house with dressed red-sandstone, thus giving the appearance of warmth which is lacking in many stone buildings.

At the beginning of the eighteenth century, Edward Parker made extensions and started developing the present 'landscape garden'.

John Parker, who died in 1754, made further additions.

Later came Thomas Lister Parker, F.S.A., who never married. A great patron of the arts, and friend of the Prince Regent. He spent a vast sum on the house, employing Jeffry Wyatt to help in the work. In 1820, feeling his creation had reached perfection, he sold Browsholme Hall with contents, and estate, to his cousin and male heir Thomas Parker of Alkincoates and Newton. The landscape gardens alone are said to have cost him over £100,000.

Many improvements were added by John William Robinson Parker, C.B., V.P.S.A., who also created the present Chapel, and on his death was succeeded by his only son Robert Parker, D.S.O., F.S.A., J.P., the present owner.

The Tudor Hall, is the main part of the communal Dining-hall, which in 1507, filled the whole centre of the ground floor, originally measuring 68 feet by 23 feet. In this room are weapons and armour from the stone-age onwards; a buck-skin coat in which one of the family was killed in 1643 at the 'Battle of Newbury', and many other treasures, including a very fine example of a court cupboard, made for the Townley family in 1590, carrying a glazed case containing thirty-three miniature figures of Monks, Nuns, and Mary of Medina, seated in a cabriole-legged chair, beneath a canopy; the chair and canopy are covered with bullion work of the late seventeenth century. Both the 'oak and the ash' are in Henry VIII, armchairs (or bobbin-chairs).

At the end of the fifteenth century, no tenant; fee-holder, or lease-holder in the Forest was allowed to keep a dog unless it was mutilated so preventing it from chasing deer. Later this law was changed and a fine imposed if anyone kept a dog too big to go through a stirrup to hunt the deer out of the corn. The Parkers of Browsholme Hall as bow-bearers of the Forest were responsible for the upholding of this law, which was never broken. The iron dog gauge or stirrup, which hangs beside a Cromwellian bracket clock, was last used in 1780.

Yes Browsholme Hall also has a skull, which is believed to be that of a Martyr of the Pilgrimage of Grace. This is kept in a court cupboard dated 1704, near the fireplace and always treated with respect until the 1850s when young Edward Parker buried it in the garden for a practical joke. Disaster quickly followed. The façade coming off walls; oak beams started smouldering, and many in the family died. In the end the terrified Edward turned confessor, and the skull was returned to the cupboard, so everything became normal again.

Also in this room can be seen an aluminium girder from the first zeppelin brought down in England in 1914-1918 war, at Cuffley.

The Drawing-room measures 40 feet by 24 feet. Here are treasures too numerous to mention, and great paintings by Sir Joshua Reynolds, Sir Peter Lely, George Romney, Sir Godfrey Kneller, one attributed to Rembrandt, and many others. How wonderful to know these beautiful things are there for all to see.

In the Dining-room are pottery and china used by the family since the reign of Queen Elizabeth I.

A tapestry on the main staircase (lower landing) is worthy of note, having been made in 1525 for King Frances I of France, and designed by Leonardo da Vinci. There is an interesting Georgian window at the end of this landing.

Many of the Regency rooms have recently been repaired under the expert guidance of Sir Albert Richardson one of our late P.R.A.s.

The Velvet Room panelling is Edwardian, by Richard Alston and his apprentice Bob Whalley. The flowered armorial frieze was painted by E. Rose, and Colonel John Parker, C.B., V.P.S.A., the father of Robert, the owner today, designed the fireplace, and together with Richard Alston carved the overmantle.

When Robert was a small boy this room was hung with velvet.

Two pictures by J. Stringer of family horses, on one of which John Parker in a carefree mood rode up the main staircase and had a 'bit of an accident'. He fortunately recovered, but the poor horse is said to haunt the house, and tradition says if its picture falls one of the family dies. (Many people believe that will happen if *any* picture falls.)

It is impossible to give an adequate description of magnificent Browsholme Hall, and all its contents can only be fully appreciated by a personal visit, and if the reader does make the effort he (or she) will be rewarded by such beauty as will remain in the memory for a long time—making you want to return again and again, until you can stand in the landscape

CHETHAM'S HOSPITAL, MANCHESTER.

CHETHAM'S HOSPITAL CLOISTERS.

CLIFTON HALL.

gardens and really feel that you are sharing the much-loved 'home' of an English gentleman.

CHETHAM'S HOSPITAL AND LIBRARY

Previously known as Thomas de la Warre's College, Chetham's Hospital in Manchester, was built about 1422, and completed about 1425 by Thomas de la Warre who was called the Priest Lord. He was last of the Norman line of the Greslets and De la Warres, and his Baron's Hall was thought to have stood on the site of the present Hall for centuries, succeeding to the manorial rights in 1398. In 1421, Thomas sought collegiate status for the Church, Royal assent was given, and Papal authority from Martin V arrived in 1426, the year Thomas de la Warre died.

The first connection of the Derby family with the College seems to have been in 1481, when James Stanley, a younger son of Thomas, the first Lord Stanley, was appointed Warden. In 1547 the College was dissolved by Edward VI, and on 9th July 1549, the Earl of Derby bought the College House from the Crown. The College was re-established by Queen Mary in 1553.

The Collegiate body in 1578 consisted of a Warden, eight fellows or chaplains, four clerks and six choristers, and was then called 'The Guild of the Blessed Virgin'. It was later dissolved again by Queen Elizabeth I and re-founded under the name of 'Christ's College' with a staff as follows: One Warden Priest, B.D., four fellows, priests B.A., two chaplains or vicars, four laymen, and four children who were skilled in music. This constitution existed until 1840, when the title of 'Warden and Fellows of the College', was changed by act of Parliament to the 'Dean and Canons of the Cathedral'. During the Civil War, buildings of the old College fell into a dilapidated condition and most of it was used as a prison.

The ancient Library was the first and only free public library in Manchester until 1850. Here are kept many treasures, and in 1870 the library of John Byrom which contains many rare books, together with the original manuscript of his carol 'Christians Awake' was given by Byrom's descendant Miss Eleanora Atherton. (See Kersal Cell).

Humphrey Chetham, (who was born in 1580, the fifth son of Henry Chetham, a wealthy Crumpsall merchant), considering the buildings to be suitable for the charitable foundation which he had in mind, entered into negotiations with the parliamentary commissioners with a view to their acquisition. His intention was later carried into effect, but unfortunately he didn't live to see them materialise, for Humphrey Chetham died at Clayton Hall in 1653, aged seventy-three, and was buried as he had wished in Chetham Chapel of the Collegiate Church in Manchester.

In 1654, his executors bought the College, and in 1656, after it had been repaired and decorated extensively in preparation, a meeting was held for the dedication of the College as 'Chetham's Hospital'.

There were then twenty-two Manchester and Salford boys between the ages of six to ten years, of 'honest, industrious and painful parents'.

This much respected man Humphrey Chetham, a bachelor, was a prosperous textile manufacturer and merchant. He declined a Knighthood in 1631, but in 1635 accepted the office of High Sheriff of Lancashire. He was a deeply religious and industrious person, and benefactor to the poor. He gave £1,000 towards the founding of the Library where there are now about sixty-five-thousand books and manuscripts in the collection.

The Chetham's Hospital buildings are of dressed stone, with walls about 3 feet thick, and roof covered in stone slates. The Great Hall is one of the finest examples of early domestic architecture in the country, and measures about 43 feet long, 24 feet wide, and 35 feet high from floor to top of the open-timbered roof. This is still called the 'Baronial Hall'.

In 1843, the first addition to the old College House included a schoolroom, and in 1878 a new school building was provided on west side of yard. The swimming-bath was built in 1898. Chetham's was partly damaged during the second World War.

Here is some interesting furniture of the Cromwellian period, including a fine walnut Queen Anne settle (1720), given by Miss Frere in 1842, from Crumpsall Hall. Two other chairs thought to be those of Catesby of the Gunpowder Plot, and known as the Catesby Chairs, bearing painted shields, are worth mentioning.

The quaint dress of Chetham boys (now only worn on ceremonial occasions) is most attractive, and takes one back to mid-seventeenth century. Chetham's is sometimes called the 'Blue Coat' school, the Tudor uniform consisting of a long belted blue coat with brass buttons, flat hat, cravat, yellow stockings and buckled shoes.

The twenty-four feoffees who maintained the founder's wishes, and the seventeen governors, decided in 1950, in association with the Ministry of Education and local authorities, to establish a school of about two-hundred-and-fifty boys, an independent Grammar School with its own junior department. This was opened in 1955. They then became known as The Combined Schools of Chetham's Hospital and Nicholls Hospital.

Discipline is still maintained, boarders rise at 6-30 a.m. and each boy is expected to do chores, which all helps to form the fine and reliable characters for which this school is noted.

For years Chetham's has provided choristers for the Manchester Cathedral Choir, and in addition has its own orchestra of fifty players.

In July 1968, this school with its great tradition behind it, was three-hundred-and-fifteen years old.

In 1969 Chetham's became Britain's first Junior School of Music, and after having previously been for boys only, became Co-educational (another step in progress which must have been a big decision to make). Tradition will still be respected in the *Girls* dress which will also be a Tudor style coat similar to the boys for important occasions. Perhaps eventually they will even join them in the Manchester Cathedral Choir.

The two-hundred girls, and two-hundred boys will need more room, so extensions are to be made to the building, and with grants of £25,000, and £5,000, offered by the Calouste Gulbenkian Foundation, and the Northern Arts and Sciences Foundation respectively, much can and *will* be done.

The School will accept suitable children from the age of seven years upwards from all over Britain and even Europe, who after being recommended by a Tutor; Headmaster, or Education Authority musical adviser, will have an audition. Pupils here shall have the maximum tuition in music possible without detracting from normal school curriculum.

CROXTETH HALL.

Below: ENTWISTLE HALL.

So Humphrey Chetham's venture expands and encourages the youth of later years to practice and appreciate another of the world's great arts—Good Music.

CLIFTON HALL

FORMERLY the residence of the family of Gaskell, Clifton Hall was originally the seat of a branch of the Hollands, from whom it passed by the marriage of Ellinor, daughter and co-heiress of Thomas Holland Esq., into the possession of Ralph Slade Gent, who again transferred it by sale, as it is supposed, to John Gaskell, an Elder in one of the Presbyterian Classes, and a man who, if report of him is to be credited, showed great indecision of character in the turbulent times of the Commonwealth, passing at one time for a Royalist, and at another for a Roundhead. In 1634, he was liberal contributor towards the erection of Trinity Church, Salford, the foundation stone of which was laid in that year by Humphrey Booth.

Nathaniel Gaskell, who died in November 1716, was father to Rebecca who married Richard Clive Esq., M.P., of Styche, and who became mother of the afterwards celebrated Lord Clive (of India).

CROXTETH HALL

CROXTETH HALL, formerly called Barrets Hall, chief seat of the Earl of Sefton, is situated in this township on the borders of Croxteth Park from which it takes its name. It was acquired by the Molyneux family in Henry VIs reign when Sir Richard Molyneux was steward of the manor, and about 1540, was a chief residence of the Molyneux family.

The oldest part of the building is the western half of the south wing, now much hidden by kitchens which were built in front of it in 1874. It is of brick with stone dressings, and mullioned windows, and has two bays projecting southward. Its date is c. 1575-1600.

The west wing was added between 1702 and 1714, and is the finest part of the building. This has a raised terrace and contains a fine set of lofty panelled rooms opening one from another, the grand staircase being at its north-east angle.

Sefton Hall, the *old* house of the Molyneux family was dismantled about 1720 and abandoned in favour of Croxteth.

The date 1693, and initials of William Molyneux are on a spout head behind the tower on the west front. There were alterations and rebuilding in 1874-7.

The present house is built round a quadrangle, its dimensions are 205 feet by 135 feet. Its chief merit lies in the early eighteenth century work and details of the panelling, but of the fittings of the *old* house little remains except a small oak door, nail studded like those at Pool Hall 1576, Moor Hall 1566, and Hale Hall c. 1600, and looking as though it were not now in its original position. Its Y-shaped iron knocker is in a curious place, near the upper hinge, and the door may be part of a large one cut down.

DUNKENHALGH HALL

DUNKENHALGH HALL, Clayton-le-Moors, Accrington, is a place of charm and elegance. The first recorded history dates as far back as 1285, but it probably existed much earlier. The owners in 1332, were the Rishtons who held it for nearly 250 years. In 1571, Dunkenhalgh Hall was sold to Thomas Walmesley, a man of the law. He had a distinguished career, and in 1580, became sergeant-at-law. In 1589, Member of Parliament for Lancashire, and the same year a judge of the Common Pleas; was knighted by James I in 1603. He enlarged the estate. His son Thomas inherited, whose son Thomas was knighted by James I at Ashton Hall, Nr Lancaster in 1617. He was M.P. for Clitheroe in 1621, and for Lancashire in 1625. Sir Thomas Walmesley died at Dunkenhalgh in 1642, and his grandson Richard succeeded while a minor. The Year after Roundhead soldiers took the house over the night before the fight at Whalley.

In 1712, the estate passed from the Walmesleys to the Petres by the marriage of Catherine Walmesley to Robert, seventh Lord Petre, who unfortunately died the following year leaving sixteen-year-old Catherine a widow with a baby son.

The castle-like building of Dunkenhalgh was largely rebuilt in the Gothic style. Oak panelling in the oak room came from Hacking Hall, Billington, which belongs to the estate. The staircase dates from early eighteenth century.

The fascinating story of the 'Dunkley Boggart' has caused many a shudder and spine-chilling thrill throughout the years. Where the River Hyndburn flows through the lower part of the grounds a small ravine can be seen. There are two bridges; one near the kitchen gardens is known as the 'Boggart Bridge'. This is where at midnight on Christmas Eve, the ghost of a young lady, dressed in a winding sheet appears. And after moving through the trees, and by the site of the bridge, vanishes. The story reveals that many years ago the Petre family employed a French lady as the children's governess, known as Lucette. One Christmas a relative of the family—a dashing young officer, fell in love with Lucette, but never intended to marry her. After gaining her affections and ruining the poor girl he left, promising to return. The unhappy Lucette dare not return to France, and was not wanted there, and she used to walk about the grounds frequented by her false lover, until her reason failed.

One wild stormy night, she wandered to the bridge under which the river rushed in torrents, and in frenzy and despair threw herself over the parapet into the surging foam.

Her brother avenged his sister's death by killing her lover in a duel.

Dunkenhalgh Hall is now an Old English Hotel, with every comfort one can require. Its 600 acres have been reduced to an area of 15 acres, but there are some beautiful trees and gardens. There are twenty-nine bedrooms all with hot and cold water. (Many have private bathrooms.) A Ballroom, Cocktail Bar, Wine Cellar, etc.

A friendly atmosphere pervades 'The Dunkenhalgh'.

ENTWISTLE HALL

NEAR the beginning of the fifteenth century when the fatal feud between Richard II, and Henry, Duke of Lancaster, son of John of Gaunt (later King Henry IV), was at full height, Entwistle Hall was the birthplace of Bertine Entwistle, who in after years rose to proud distinction, and was knighted by King Henry

EXTWISTLE HALL.

V, under whose successful banner Sir Bertine proved himself an accomplished and gallant warrior. The bravery and loyalty of Sir Bertine Entwistle forms the subject of a stirring ballad, consisting of about 21 verses, in Roby's 'Traditions of Lancashire', which commence thus:

The Brave Sir Bertine Entwisel
Hath donned his coat of steel,
And left his hall and stately home
To fight for England's weal.

To fight for England's weal, I trow
And good King Harry's right,
His loyal heart was warm and true,
His sword and buckler bright.

Sir Bertine died without issue, and the property passed into the hands of another branch of the same family, who resided there until the sixteenth century.

In 1555 the whole estates in the district belonging to Entwistles, came 'by casual means' into the hands of another old Lancashire family Edward Tyldesley Esq., of Tyldesley and Morleys. After four generations the manor passed by purchase to several of his tenants. One John Kay was fortunate in securing the lands immediately connected to the hall, and also the mansion itself. It is believed that a new building was erected in the first half of the seventeenth century.

Since the nineteenth century the hall has been used as a farm, and is still in existence.

EXTWISTLE HALL

Standing on a high ridge, between the valleys of the Don and Swinden water, about three miles from the village of Worsthorne in Briercliffe, Burnley, is the tall building of Extwistle Hall. Facing North frontwards, the ground slopes towards the back south side where a basement makes the house have four storeys.

From this bleak commanding situation there is a similarity to the 'Wuthering Heights' of Brontë fame, especially when the howling winter wind rages, and torrential rain lashes against the mullioned windows. Extwistle Hall is built of local gritstone, with stone-slated roofs, and is a rectangular block measuring 34 feet by 27 feet 6 inches, with a lower two storey building with plain gabled roof on the east end. In the early nineteenth century a former west wing collapsed destroying some of the best rooms. This Hall has a massive chimney which projects 5 feet, with a width of 15 feet. A small flagged courtyard at front of building measures 43 by 33 feet. The North side has a high fence wall with moulded coping, and balled gate-piers fronting the road, give an impressive appearance. The Great Hall measures 24 feet by 21 feet, and is at the eastern end of the main block. Approaching this from the forecourt up the wide flight of stone steps some of the true beauty of Extwistle Hall presents itself. The Entrance was in the north-west corner through a striking four-centred doorway which has a label with square panel above, but unfortunately this is now bricked up. The north wall with its high ten light mullioned window with double transoms and hood mould, remains in its original state.

The south wall of the Hall inside is occupied almost completely by a Tudor arched fireplace which is unfortunately bricked up. Above this remains a fragment of ornamental plaster-work bearing the intriguing words: CRAS (Tomorrow) NESCIO (Not to Know) CUIVS (Whose) . . . (All this is mine today—tomorrow, Who knows?) The staircase is of stone. The north-west wing is probably seventeenth century and less austere than the main block, this reaches to the four storeys and is of equal height with the Great Hall. Although Extwistle Hall has suffered much wear and tear over the centuries it still remains a splendid example of an Elizabethan Squire's Mansion, with a large amount of the original structure standing.

The Parker family can be traced as far back as 1333, to Johannes Parcarius of Brunley, who had a son Adam le Parker, whose son William le Parker followed. Later, during the reign of Henry VIII, in 1510, John Parker, gent, held Moncke Hall in Extwistle, and lands in Briercliffe by knight's service. His son and heir John Parker succeeded in 1529 when aged forty-eight, was married about 1526-1528 to Isabella, daughter of John Brockholes. *He* was succeeded by his son Robert Parker, who purchased under authority of the Royal licence, from William Ramsden, the manor of Briercliffe and Extwistle, to be held of the king by the service of the sixtieth part of one Knight's fee* and the annual payment of eight-shillings. Robert married Jane or (Joan) Haydok, of Haydok.

John, the son and heir of Robert, married Margaret, daughter of Lawrence Townley, of Burnside, Esq., great-grandson of John Townley of Townley, Esq. They had fourteen children, three named Robert.

In 1561, the Byre Law of Extwistle was confirmed by John Townley of Townley: John Parker of Extwistle, and others. About the same year Extwistle Hall was built, by the same John Parker who died in 1635, holding at the same time Extwistle Hall, Monk Hall, and various lands in the township. This John had refused a knighthood in 1631, for which he paid a fine of fifteen pounds.

The last of the family to live at Extwistle Hall was Robert Parker of Extwistle, Esq. Born in 1663, he was High Sheriff of Lancaster in 1710, and married Elizabeth, daughter and co-heiress of Christopher Banastre of Banke Hall, Bretherton, Nr Preston, by whom he obtained Cuerden. A keen huntsman, he kept a 'Journal of Events' describing the days he went hunting—killing hares. Alas, the hares were not the only sufferers to be killed. On one of these expeditions Robert Parker 'The Old Squire' was over ambitious. The date was Thursday 20th March 1717-18. In teeming rain which had soaked the gunpowder from the gun into his clothes, he returned home, and unfortunately, while drying out, an explosion occurred which injured him so badly that he died the following day. Two of his daughters were also hurt. The rooms of one wing were extensively damaged, and a staircase leading to a blocked up door appears to have led into that wing which no longer exists.

During 1666, Extwistle Hall was said to have eleven hearths (for the hearth tax) and there were a total of 122 in the township.

A sister of Robert Parker, Jane, married Edward Parker, of Brownsholme in 1693. The next heir was Banastre Parker, of Cuerden and Extwistle, Esq., born in 1697. He married Anne, daughter and co-heiress of

---

* KNIGHT'S FEE: As much inheritance as is sufficient to maintain a knight with convenient revenues. In those days about eight-hundred acres.

FLETCHER
MOSS MUSEUM.

FOXDENTON
HALL.

William Clayton, of Preston, and of Liverpool where he was M.P. for the borough. Banastre went to live at Cuerden Hall, Nr Preston after his father's death.

Their eldest son Robert Parker Esq., of Cuerden, born 1727, succeeded. He married Anne, daughter and heiress of Thomas Townley Esq., of Royle.

Thomas Townley Parker Esq., of Cuerden, succeeded his brother Banastre. Born in 1760, he was married at Croston in 1787, to Susanna, daughter of Peter Brooke Esq., of Astley and Charnock. Thomas Townley Parker was High Sheriff of Lancaster in 1793. There were four children of the marriage—one son, Robert Townley Parker Esq., who succeeded. He was born at Cuerden Hall 27th August 1793, was High Sheriff of Lancashire 1817, Deputy Lieutenant, and J.P., M.P. for Preston in first Parliament of Queen Victoria, and again in 1852. In 1816 married Harriet, youngest daughter of Thomas Brooke Esq., of Chester. They had eight children—five sons and three daughters, the heir apparent being the eldest son Thomas Townley Parker Esq., of Charnock, who was born at Cuerden 5th May 1822, and became J.P. for Lancaster.

Canon Arthur Townley Parker who died in 1902, was a highly respected rector of Burnley Parish Church for many years, and also the owner of the advowson, which he transferred to the Bishop of Manchester by an Act of Parliament. Canon Parker was High Sheriff of Lancashire in 1817, Member of Parliament for Preston from 1837-1841, and again from 1852-1857. He was Guild Mayor of Preston in 1862—an office which his grandfather Robert Parker had held in 1762.

The son of Robert Townley Parker (who died in 1879), succeeded. Thomas Townley Parker assumed the name and arms of Townley in addition to the family name and arms of Parker. He died in 1906, leaving all his estates, including Extwistle Hall to his nephew Reginald Arthur Tatton of Cuerden.

Across a field behind Extwistle Hall are extensive remains of the Extwistle Hall Estate Mill, built by John Parker about 1605, as the Estate Corn Mills. Many years later these mills were run by William Parker, born 1730, who died at Lea Green House, Near Extwistle in 1816. Mr I. J. Thompson, of Whalley, Near Blackburn, who gave additional information on this Hall, is an actual descendant of this William Parker. Daniel Parker, the son of William, also ran the mills which by then were thought to be functioning for the manufacture of worsted. He introduced the spinning of cotton to the mill, and was joined in the business by his son William, who was born in 1788, but who was unfortunately drowned in the mill dam in an attempt to rescue a servant. Daniel Parker was then joined by his other son Peter Parker (1794-1858), and another son John Parker, born 1799.

Among the ruins of this old mill are underground passages, and some large stone blocks originally used for machinery water wheel beds, and in which the spindle sockets and bolt holes remain.

Extwistle Hall has been used as a farmhouse for about two centuries, and although of lonely appearance the building is far from deserted, for the present owner Mr Wilfred Heap, of Hapton, Nr Burnley, having spent much effort and money on restoration, has let it to tenant farmer Mr Robert Kirkham, whose friend Mr Geoffrey Stott, of Shuttleworth, Ramsbottom, has kindly assisted a great deal in research for this residence.

A ghost known as 'Fair Alice' used to frequent these premises but no one has been aware of her presence for many years. Who knows? perhaps the spirit of 'The Owd Squire' still lingers within these strong windswept walls which have protected so many people and withstood the centuries of storm and strife.

So stands the tall proud edifice of Extwistle Hall, a stark reminder of the past.

FLETCHER MOSS MUSEUM

KNOWN as the 'Old Parsonage', this house stands in Wilmslow Road, Didsbury, and is a fascinating late Georgian and early Victorian building with an interesting story. It was opened as a branch gallery in 1923, housing the best of the City Art Gallery's collection of water-colours, from Paul Sandby to the present day, including a group by J. M. W. Turner. There is also porcelain of early nineteenth century.

Once the loved home of Alderman Fletcher Moss J.P., who cherished every stick, stone, and square yard of land, this house was full of happy memories for him. As the old song says:

'Mid pleasures and palaces though we may roam,
Be it ever so humble, there's no place like home.'*

Alderman Moss believed this with all his heart, and to quote his own words: 'It is better to dwell in an old house with the ghosts, than in a new house where you can hear your neighbour's pianos.'

Despite the years, Fletcher Moss Museum still retains a humble atmosphere, and to quote again, from Alderman Moss's fourth book: 'It helps us to feel our share in the heritage of trouble or joy from those who have gone before us if we learn some little of what has happened in these old homes. We may listen to the folk-lore, and ponder over the book lore "many a quaint and curious volume of forgotten lore", as the grandfather's clocks slowly tick out the passing hours of the long dark nights of winter, and the ghosts of the departed hover around. All houses wherein men have lived and died are haunted though the stranger cannot see the ghosts, the old folks living in the houses see. Old tales are told again: tales of love and hate, jealousy and treachery, of never ending feud, of battle, murder, and sudden death. Death on the scaffold or in prison, death to the innocent as well as to the guilty, and sometimes there are dim records of happy life that has no history. Some faded memorial of quiet peace and life-long love that is all forgottten.'

How very appropriate these words are for all ancient houses, and they are the things I have endeavoured to describe in this book.

Alderman Moss J.P., the son of John Moss, a corn merchant, of Hanging Ditch, was born at Ryecroft House, Cheetham Hill, Manchester, in 1843. His mother was a daughter of Joseph and Mary Fletcher, of New Cross. They were descended from an old Didsbury family. His father Mr John Moss was born at Mees Hall, Staffordshire, and when a young man went to live in Manchester to learn the corn merchants business at 'Messrs Joseph Fletcher

* Home Sweet Home was composed by American actor John Howard Payne (Born 1792—died 1852). In 1823, he produced an opera in London in which the song was first sung.

HAIGH HALL.

HAIGH HALL.   Old Print 1832.

23

and Co,' of New Cross. Joseph Fletcher had three children, John, Hannah, and Catherine. When his father died John carried on the business with the help of John Moss who had married his sister Catherine. The business was moved to Hanging Ditch. John Fletcher died in 1838, unmarried, and John Moss became head of the firm Fletcher & Co. He was later elected Chairman of Manchester Corn Exchange, and was a Churchwarden of Didsbury 1855-6. Leaving Ryecroft House he went to live at 'The Elms', Didsbury, adjoining the Parsonage. Later, in 1865, he removed to the Old Parsonage, where he died in 1867. After having lived there about twenty years, making a wise decision Mr Fletcher Moss bought the house and property, living there fifty-four years from 1865 until December 26th 1919, (the day he died). He was buried in Cheadle Cemetery on January 2nd 1920.

The Old Parsonage was connected with Didsbury Chappell or Church, and built about 1282. It no doubt passed through the hands of various Lords of the Manor: the Gresleys, La Warres, Wests, Lacys and Mosleys. Sir Nicholas Mosley who was Lord Mayor of London in 1599, was buried at Didsbury in 1612. About 1620, the original Chappell was almost completely demolished and rebuilt of stone in a style of Gothic architecture.

In 1726, the advowson came into the possession of Lady Anne Bland, a daughter of Sir Edward Mosley, of Hulme Hall. She died in 1736. In 1829, it was purchased by William Newall, and changed hands a few times which caused a scandal in the Parish.

This Chappell had been Roman Catholic for 300 years but not dedicated to any saint. It was, however, eventually dedicated to St James.

There must have been a Priest's house much earlier, but it wasn't until 1646, that one was actually known to exist, although Church records begin about 1562. The Parson before 1646 was Mr Clayton, he was then referred to as the Minister, but at other times would be called the Priest. He was considered rich on forty pounds a year.

The present Parsonage was no doubt built on the site and partly from the remains of an older one, but the early history is somewhat obscure as no old deeds could be traced. The title to this place began with an Act of Parliament of 1786, re the estates of the Bamfords of Bamford who'd inherited from John Davenport of Stockport. (This probably being a part.) The Act cost William Bamford £550, and to raise sufficient money he sold an Inn known as the 'Cock', a barn, and three small houses, also land, to Sam Bethall, a joiner, to repair or erect better buildings, and pay a chief rent to the Countess of Dundonald who inherited the Bamford-Hesketh estates. In 1804, Bethell sold out for £1,250, and in 1832 the property was sold for £2,450, to Richard Fletcher of Birch Hall, and William Newall. They sold it to Louisa Titley, who made it over to trustees. She married the Reverend Sam Newall, curate of Didsbury, and son of William Newall. Louisa Titley died shortly after, and the Parson left but kept the property, repairing it and adding two rooms. He left because the house was haunted.

A lawyer bought the advowson and presented the Rev. W. J. Kidd, (who had married his sister) as Parson. Rev. W. J. Kidd remained in the house ten years, which he rented from Newall, but constantly haunted by ghosts he eventually left and had a new Rectory built some distance from the Church.

In 1884, Mr Fletcher Moss bought the Old Parsonage for £4,000, and although the ghosts were often disturbing he learned to *live* with them. For here was a man who could see beauty, and had great compassion.

At one time a village smithy stood opposite the Parsonage, together with a few houses, and thatched cottages.

The front door of the Parsonage was made from massive oak shelves from the dairy at Broad Oak Farm. Mr Fletcher Moss made the knocker from an oak tree growing in his field. This was designed after the knocker on the oldest door of Dunster Castle. The design of the Gothic tracery came from Glastonbury. The Eagle doorway in the garden wall was brought from the Spread Eagle Hotel, Corporation Street, Manchester. Mr Fletcher Moss bought it as a souvenir for ten pounds when the Hotel was demolished, he himself having once been the proprietor. It cost him £80 for transport and re-erection.

Human bones have been discovered in the grounds at various times, one of these was a jaw-bone which Mr Moss thought may have belonged to a local female being rather worn at the hinges (keen sense of humour).

The Parsonage has a beautiful Old English Garden which is now a haven of rest and recreation for its many visitors. Mr Fletcher Moss thought many of the plants may have been planted by Priests or Monks the names being appropriately selected: Madonna Lily, Star-of-Bethlehem, Monks Hood, Solomon's Seal, Aaron's Rod, Balm, Herb of Grace, or Rue, Lenten Lilies, etc. The Linden trees were planted by Captain Webster in 1827, and a large Weeping Ash by Parson Newall about 1837. Under this tree Mr Moss buried much-loved dogs and a favourite mare. Each having its own small headstone, for Mr Fletcher Moss loved:

'All things bright and beautiful,
All creatures great and small . . .'

This great, and kindly gentleman left his beloved home for the citizens and public, under the control of Manchester Corporation, with the hope that it would be kept as a reminder of what a comfortable home in olden times was like to future generations. In his own words:

'Light be the hand of ruin laid,
Upon the home I love.'

It was impossible to keep every stick and stone exactly as it was in Mr Moss's day, but the Museum is in excellent hands and couldn't be used to a better purpose than to display some of the most beautiful works of art in the City. In this way Alderman Fletcher Moss J.P., has done Lancashire a great service, and one of his sincerest wishes has been fulfilled, and still *will* be fulfilled in that all who enter those walls should find Rest, and Peace.

FOXDENTON HALL

FOXDENTON HALL as seen today is very picturesque in its beautiful setting of gardens which in summertime are a glorious mass of colour, wide lawns and stately trees, and within its comparatively small park makes a pleasant retreat from the town although quite

GAWTHORPE HALL.

HALL-I' TH'-WOOD.

close. There are bowling greens, football pitches, and even a pets corner.

The first owners of the original Foxdenton Hall were the de Traffords. In 1215 Richard de Trafford conferred the manor and lordship of Chadderton upon Geoffrey his second son who assumed the name Chadderton. His great grand-daughter Margaret married John de Radclyffe the grandson of Richard de Radclyffe, of Radclyffe Tower and Foxdenton, and the Hall passed as a dowry into the Radclyffe family.

In 1620 William Radclyffe built a second Hall on the site of the old one, this was described as 'a noble and lofty edifice' and was built in the half-timbered style.

Sir William Radclyffe and his heir were loyal supporters of King Charles I, and in 1642 fought in the battle of Edgehill where they both lost their lives. The second son also named William, known as 'The Foxdenton Redhead' because of his hair colouring, fought at Lostwithiel and was knighted on the battlefield for gallantry, but through supporting the king's cause nearly lost his lands.

Later, about 1698, Alexander Radclyffe inherited. He pulled the house down which Sir William had built, and erected the present Hall which is in the classic Renaissance style. Alexander the quiet reserved gentleman died in 1735.

Robert Radclyffe was the last of the Radclyffes to be born at Foxdenton; a close friend of the Prince of Wales (afterwards George III) much of his time was spent at Court.

Foxdenton Hall was owned by the Radclyffes for many years, but in 1922 the Hall and grounds were leased to the Chadderton Urban District Council and it was opened to the public. In 1960 the Council purchased it and in 1963 decided to restore the building. This was completed in 1965.

William Radclyffe's old stone house built in 1620 is however still partly in evidence, for it forms the basement of the present Hall today with its mullioned windows. The present house is a striking example of its time, with central entrance and rooms at each side. The wall panelling in the Entrance Hall dates from 1620 and the rest from 1700. Here on the ceiling are the original oak beams. There is a fine oak staircase which is typical of buildings by Christopher Wren. The middle eighteenth century Chimney Pieces in the panelled rooms are still in excellent condition with their ornate plasterwork and lend a charm of their own.

No alterations have been made to the plan since 1750.

The Council have made an excellent job of restoring the early Georgian panelled rooms, and today Foxdenton Hall is a very important cultural and social centre in Chadderton.

GAWTHORPE HALL

AN impressive castle-like building, Gawthorpe Hall stands about half-way between Burnley and Padiham, and from its position in a very fine park, has a lovely view across the River Calder, of the haunt of famous 'Lancashire Witches', Pendle Hill.

This fine example of a late Elizabethan House was built around three sides of a much older Pele tower, with stone walls eight feet thick. The restoration of the building was entrusted to Sir Charles Barry in 1849, who raised both tower and chimneys to give greater boldness in the sky line, and surrounded the Hall with a pierced parapet of the Elizabethan style.

The main entrance is in the centre of the façade, and in the Great Hall, which measures about 36 feet long and 21 feet wide with flat ceiling, is a minstrel's gallery. There is also a striking Ingle-Nook here.

The Long Gallery, which was probably originally intended to be used as a dancing-room, is 72 feet in length, and has three Elizabethan bays and seven large windows. This is at the top of the building.

The Drawing Room was built in 1603. In the plaster work here are figures of Sir Richard Shuttleworth Kt., and his wife, above the fireplace. The grandfather clock is one of the earliest known. Original plaster ceilings and panellings can be seen in many rooms, also original furniture.

Adjoining the Hall is a fine barn constructed with massive timbers.

Gawthorpe Hall has been the home of the Shuttleworth family since 1330, when Agnes, daughter and heiress of William de Hacking, conveyed it to her husband Ughtred, son of Henry de Shuttleworth. From him the estate descended uninterruptedly to Robert Shuttleworth, of Barton Lodge Esq., who died in 1816, and by will dated 1815, gave all his Manors and lands in both Lancashire and Westmorland in trust to John, Lord Crewe, and Abraham Henry Chambers, of Bond Street, Middlesex Esq., for the use of his second son Robert Shuttleworth Esq., Barrister-at-Law, and Chairman of the Quarter Sessions at Preston, who in the year 1816, in Edinburgh, married Janet, daughter of Sir John Marjoribanks Bart., of Lees, in Berwickshire, and died in 1818, having willed his estates to his only child Janet Shuttleworth, who was then not even one-year-old. In 1842 she married James Phillips Kay, Esq., M.D., who assumed the surname and arms of Shuttleworth.

The widow of Robert Shuttleworth Esq., married Frederick North, of Hastings Esq.

Members of the family fought in the Civil Wars, also first and second World Wars, and many have had a seat in Parliament. They have done a great amount for the progress of Education and Welfare. Lord Shuttleworth of Leck Hall, permitted the use of Gawthorpe as a cultural centre, and the 'Gawthorpe Foundation' was formed about 1955, with this in mind, being named thus two years later when with emphasis on the Arts and Crafts, educational courses were arranged on Drama, Music, Geology, also lectures and demonstrations, and with the encouragement of Manchester University; Practical help from the Education Department of the Lancashire County Council, and official bodies and others, including the approval of the National Trust and their requirement that the Hall should be put to good use, this was carried forth, with patrons the Right Hon. the Earl of Derby, M.C.; the Right Hon. the Lord Shuttleworth, M.C., M.A., D.L., J.P.; County Alderman Sir Alfred Bates, M.C., D.L.; County Alderman Sir Andrew Smith, C.B.E., J.P.; The Vice-Chancellors of the Universities of Lancaster, Leeds, Liverpool, Manchester and Sheffield; The Chairman of the Lancashire County Council; The Committee Chairman being Colonel Robert Parker, D.S.O., F.S.A., J.P., of Browsholme Hall, Clitheroe. And the Organizing Secretary Commander James Pearson, R.N., of Fulwood, Preston.

Gawthorpe Hall, owned by Lord Shuttleworth, becoming the property of the National Trust about

HEATON HALL, MANCHESTER.

HOGHTON TOWER.
Old Print.

27

1970, will then be leased to the Lancashire County Council for the use of their Education Committee, primarily to provide accommodation for the Rachel Kay-Shuttleworth collections of textiles and their active use. Gawthorpe Hall houses a vast treasure trove gathered from all over the world by the very great Lady the Hon. Rachel B. Kay-Shuttleworth, M.B.E., J.P., who lived at the Hall most of her life. Her knowledge of textiles was incredible. Among these treasures are woven printed fabrics, some of the most exquisite embroidery, and lace as delicate as gossamer. Here are many rare pieces: Chinese Emperor's Robes; Court Robes; Queen Anne and Jacobean bedspreads; there are even embroideries worked with pure gold and silver threads. In another section can be seen a picture embroidered with hair.

The Costume section includes embroidered shirts for gentlemen dating from 1780 (of course they were even more vain then, than today), Victorian Wedding Dresses in silk etc. There is a section of furnishing materials, and a superb collection of 'White Work' which includes a dress worn by Queen Victoria when she was a tiny one-year-old.

An interesting Library is available to students, teachers, and technicians etc.

Miss Kay-Shuttleworth, 'Our Rachel' as she is affectionately called, was truly a remarkable person, who spent most of her life in collecting these treasures, and indeed creating them herself, as well as teaching others to do so. Her work can be seen at Gawthorpe Hall, and no doubt that in years to come this too will be priceless. Rachel's enthusiasm was shared by all who met her, and it is with sadness that we recall her death in 1967. But her wonderful personality will live on in all the beautiful work, and treasures.

As Rachel Kay-Shuttleworth herself said so often, we must: 'Cherish the Past; Adorn the Present, and Create for the Future.' Thus we shall also cherish her memory.

HAIGH HALL

A HALL which could be called 'down to earth' its owners having been connected with various forms of mining, the windows of Haigh Hall overlook a park of 122 acres as far as the canal, and lower plantations of 103 acres, being $21\frac{1}{2}$ acres within the Wigan County Borough boundary, home town of the well-known artist Theodore Major.

Haigh Hall was built about 1830-49 on the site of a much older house. The old English word Haigh means enclosure, which in Anglo-Saxon times could have been a clearing in a forest where the people lived and cattle grazed.

As far back as 1188 the manor of Haigh was held by Hugh le Norreys then by his grandson of the same name, whose daughter Mabel inherited about 1295. She was married to Sir William de Bradshaigh. These were hard times when even the lord of the manor didn't have a really comfortable easy chair.

People throughout the years have been fascinated with the 'Legend of Mab's Cross' which used to stand at Wigan Parish Church, Standishgate, but was later moved into the grounds of the Girls' High School.

Sir William Bradshaigh, second son of Sir John, was a great traveller and soldier. After he'd been away for over seven years in the wars, Mabel, thinking he was dead, married a Welsh knight. Sir William returned in 1322 in palmer's dress among the poor to Haigh, and Mabel thinking how much he resembled her former husband wept bitterly. Her present husband the knight was angry, so Sir William revealed his identity and the knight fled. Sir William followed and slew him at Newton-le-Willows.

Dame Mabel was made to do penance by walking barefoot once a week from Haigh to the cross at Wigan Church for as long as she lived, thus it became known as Mab's Cross. What a job for a chiropodist.

Sir William was outlawed for a year and a day for killing the knight, but he and Mabel lived happily ever after until Sir William died.

Sir William's long absence may partly have been that he was a prisoner. The Earl of Lancaster's favourite Sir Robert de Holland acted as the Earl's representative in the County, granting pardons or sentencing people to death as he wished arousing much hatred and jealousy among the gentry, who with Sir William banded together under the leadership of Sir Adam Banastre. They staged a revolt. Sir Henry de Bury was killed, and after an enquiry some of the offenders were hanged and Sir William outlawed for failing to turn up at court. Sir Adam and friends with eight-hundred men went raiding and pillaging round the county until a force was sent by the sheriff. Some leaders were killed, and Sir Adam fled but was betrayed and Sir William escaped. He was pardoned in 1318 but probably thought it wiser to keep away from Haigh while the enemy were so powerful.

Sir William returned in 1322, after the Earl of Lancaster's execution, and Sir Robert de Holland was imprisoned. But in those times it was a case of an eye for an eye, and blood for blood and Sir William was often involved in civil disturbances—if you could call them 'civil' and during one of these was killed at the very spot where he was said to have killed the knight.

On Dame Mabel's death Haigh Hall became the property of Sir William's nephew. Mabel's ghost was said to haunt a gallery at the Hall, which was known as Mab's gallery. Both Sir William and Dame Mabel were buried in Wigan Parish Church, after a stormy life.

Sir Roger Bradshaigh born about 1628 inherited in 1641 on the death of his grandfather. Charles II landed in Scotland in 1650, when several suspected Royalists including Sir Roger were arrested. He was released on a promise not to help the Royalists. The Earl of Derby was defeated in an attempt to raise Lancashire for the King by Parliamentary forces, Sir Roger rescued Sir William Throgmorton taking him to Haigh where he recovered. Sir Thomas Tyldesley of Leigh was killed in this battle, the monument in Wigan Lane was built in his memory.

When James, seventh Earl of Derby, was beheaded in 1651, his body was at Haigh overnight before being buried at Ormskirk.

At the Restoration Wigan's loyalty to the Royalist cause was acknowledged by Charles II, he granted a new Borough Charter and sword of honour to the town. Sir Roger Bradshaigh was the Mayor of Wigan and is named in the Charter.

The Bradshaighs produced cannel which is a gas-producing fuel like polished black marble, and derives its name from the candle from the way it burns. Sir Roger Bradshaigh spent much time in developing his cannel mines. John Dwight who was at one time secretary to the Bishops of Chester used to experi-

HOGHTON TOWER.

HOGHTON TOWER.
Old Print.

ment with the clay from the Haigh pits, and took out patents for porcelain in 1671 and 1684, and claimed to be the first maker in England, so Sir Roger evidently made that possible too. He'd certainly gone into the business whole-heartedly investing all his money in it, so that when he died in 1684, and his son also died in 1686, the family were in rather a bad way financially.

Cannel was a remarkable material and was used for a wide variety of purposes; Portrait busts, teapots, sugar-basins, and in the seventeenth century even a summer-house was built of it, this was still standing in the nineteenth century when the great Sir Walter Scott visited Haigh.

An Elizabethan façade was added to old Haigh Hall and a carved door, these were attributed to Inigo Jones.

From 1549 until 1770 the lord of Haigh was named Roger Bradshaigh, the last Sir Roger died in 1770 and his sister's grand-daughter Elizabeth Dalrymple inherited at the age of ten. When twenty she married Alexander Lindsay the twenty-third Earl of Crawford.

At this time Haigh Hall had been unoccupied for ten years and was suffering from subsidence, it was unfurnished and the mines were derelict. The Earl at the age of fourteen had succeeded to the estate at Balcarres which was heavily mortgaged and there were nine brothers and sisters to support. He determined to save Haigh and apart from the time when he was Governor of Jamaica spent much money and time in the effort. He sold Balcarres to his brother, and knowing very little about coal, studied the subject, the markets and transport. The Leeds-Liverpool Canal conveniently ran through his own grounds, and he purchased no less than thirty-three boats and barges.

On his return from Jamaica in 1801 the Earl was exempt from army service being lame through an accident, yet when Napoleon threatened to invade England he became leader of the Wigan Loyal Volunteers.

Earl Alexander started the Haigh Ironworks in 1790 to manufacture colliery machinery. They eventually supplied other pits, and under the supervision of Mr Robert Daglish in 1812 made the first locomotive to be used in Lancashire, its purpose being to convey coal at Orrell colliery. It could pull twenty wagons each holding a ton and was known as Daglish's Walking Horse.

In 1835, James, twenty-fourth Earl of Crawford, finding himself unable to keep the ironworks going, leased them for twenty-one years, and the name became the Haigh Foundry Company. In 1884 the works closed down.

Haigh Foundry were the makers of the cast iron tubing and arches for the first railway Mersey tunnel, and also the Laxey Wheel in the Isle of Man, which was made to pump water out of the lead mines at Laxey. They were 1,800 feet deep. The wheel measured 226 feet in circumference, and 6 feet thick. It took about one-hundred draught horses borrowed from local farmers to pull it up the steep road from the foundry. This was an important occasion, Tom Sharrock went from Haigh Foundry to supervise the erection by Mr R. Casement, the superintendent engineer of the Great Laxey Mines Company. Lady Isabella Hope, wife of the Governor of the Isle-of-Man in 1854, set the wheel in motion and it was named Isabella. In 1930 the wheel suffered damage

through floods. The mines are no longer in use but the Great Wheel was reconditioned and people allowed to climb up and admire the view. It is now a source of interest for holiday makers.

The present Haigh Hall was built by James, who became the twenty-fourth Earl of Crawford in 1825, and was created Baron Wigan of Haigh Hall. This Hall was built on the site of the old one. The Earl lived in Park Cottages during the time and people named him Jimmy in the Trees. Well he certainly didn't have his head in the clouds, drawing the plans himself and directing procedures. The impressive square block is built round a small courtyard, and is of a hard sandstone obtained from Parbold quarries, brought by canal and dressed on the spot by John Haig a Scots apprentice. The supply of this stone being short the top part of building is different. The iron work came from the Haigh Foundry and there are doors of fumed oak from the estate while doorways and surrounds are from the Earls Jamaican plantations. The only materials which didn't come from the estates are those from the marble fireplaces and plaster ceilings. So Wigan people can be proud of the fact that Haigh Hall is nearly all home-made. Industrious Industrial Lancashire. There's a staircase, gallery, and three-arched arcade that were built by Wigan woodcarver Tim Runnigar at a cost of £50 during the reign of Queen Anne. The 40 miles of paths in the plantations were made during the Lancashire cotton famine in 1861-3 to give employment. Earl James was a generous and popular man. He died in 1869, and his son Alexander the twenty-fifth Earl succeeded.

In 1873, King Edward VII and Queen Alexandra, then Prince and Princess of Wales, stayed at Haigh Hall. Great preparations were made and the whole place decorated at a cost of £80,000. Italian curtains, crimson and black Indian carpets, Spanish chairs in leather and gold, other chairs of silk and gold. There were exotic plants everywhere and flowers. The boudoir for the princess had Persian carpets and was decorated in white and gold. The Drawing Room had Persian and Turkey carpets, and specially woven curtains from France; eighty paintings by Old Masters: Botticelli, Van Dyke, Sir Joshua Reynolds and many others. The drive was decorated with banners sent from Florence. It must have been a magnificent sight and an unforgettable occasion.

The Estate was self-supporting in food also with its own dairy produce, vegetables, poultry and meat. The Earl had forty farms on the estate managed by a bailiff, these were later let to tenant farmers but the Home Farm continued to supply the family.

The twenty-fifth Earl, Alexander, was a scholar, author, traveller, and book-lover. He wrote philosophy, history, and art criticism, and translated ancient manuscripts dating from the sixth century, some even written on the bark of trees. His was thought to have been the best private library in the country, but unfortunately there are no longer any books or art treasures at Haigh Hall.

Earl Alexander died in Florence in 1880, and his son Ludovic inherited as the twenty-sixth Earl of Crawford. In the same year he sold some valuable possessions, the mines were badly affected due to the trade slump, but in 1886 the Earl acquired Balcarres from an uncle—his mother's brother. She was a grand-daughter of Robert Lindsay who originally bought it from his brother.

Earl Ludovic was an astronomer and wrote books

HOLKER HALL.

Painting, Margaret Chapman.

on the subject. Also a yachtsman he travelled far and wide for scientific purposes. He was succeeded by his son David the twenty-seventh Earl of Crawford who died in 1940.

The library which was the personal property of the Earl of Crawford was disposed of before he sold the Hall.

During the first and second world wars Haigh Hall was used as a hospital. Bombs actually landed in the grounds 'down to earth' obviously but most unwelcome.

In 1947, Haigh Hall and grounds were purchased by Wigan Corporation and for some time the Hall was used for exhibition purposes, but now the main rooms are leased to a private caterer and are mostly used for wedding parties. A superb setting, and so the sound of happy laughter echoes through this old Hall.

HALL-I' TH'-WOOD

ABOUT 1½ miles from Bolton on a steep river cliff stands this interesting Manor House, part of which is of the beautiful wood and plaster half-timbered structure dating back to the fifteenth century. This Hall was built by Lawrence Brownlow whose great-grandson of the same name in 1591 added a Withdrawing-Room, Bedroom, and Loft of local stone. Shortly afterwards being in rather difficult circumstances financially, the Brownlows sold the Hall to Christopher Norris, a Bolton clothier, who was helped by his son Alexander with a loan of £2,000.

Alexander Norris succeeded in 1639. He was a Puritan, and handled the confiscated estates of the Royalists in the County at the time of the Civil War. Alexander demolished the west side of the building, and added the south-west wing in dressed stone with deep mullioned windows. He also built the porch in 1648.

Hall-i' th'-Wood shows clearly the different styles of building over two progressive centuries with no subsequent additions after the middle seventeenth century.

The estate including over 1,761 acres of land passed to Alice, daughter of Alexander Norris, who married John Starkey Esq., of Huntroyde in about 1654, with the Hall as part of her marriage settlement. It was next owned by their son Le Gendre P. Starkey Esq., but in the eighteenth century was unoccupied until let as tenements.

Hall-i' th'-Wood became the home of Samuel Crompton who was born in 1753, at a farm in Firwood Fold, Tonge, the house still being preserved as an Ancient Monument. After her husband George Crompton died, Mrs Crompton obtained lease of Hall-i' th'-Wood in 1764, and here Samuel lived in what he described as a large old mansion with a number of spare rooms which he could take for his own use, having only mother and two sisters to occupy the whole. His mother had a hard time making ends meet but was determined Samuel's education wouldn't be affected, sending him to school and evening classes until he was sixteen, although earlier when ten years of age he was placed out for a year to learn weaving. This was no doubt helpful to him in later years.

In 1779, realizing the poor quality of warp produced by the Household Jenny he created the machine known as the 'mule', used in the manufacture of cotton, this was worked by hand. In 1812, Parliament granted Samuel Crompton the sum of £5,000 for his invention, and in 1842 his children received £200, from the Royal Bounty Fund.

Samuel Crompton was a musician also, and here at Hall-i' th'-Wood is the actual chamber organ which he played at choir practices in Bury Street, Swedenborgion Chapel where he was choir-master. He was also a writer of music, and several of his compositions can be seen including a hymn written to celebrate George IIIs Jubilee. Without doubt Samuel Crompton was a remarkable person, and brilliant man.

The Cromptons left Hall-i' th'-Wood in 1782, it was later occupied by tenant farmers successively. It was in a bad state of disrepair when the first Viscount Leverhulme, of Bolton bought it in 1898, and after much time and energy spent on its restoration he presented the Hall to the Corporation of Bolton in 1900. Later he presented much of the present furnishings for a Folk Museum, to show something of how a well-to-do yeoman family lived many years ago.

In the Main Hall the stone fireplace dates from 1648 when the Norris wing was added. The furniture here is mainly seventeenth century. Hall-i' th'-Wood has a lovely oak staircase also dated 1648.

In Room 4, (the Bed-Chamber which was built by Lawrence Brownlow in 1591), there is oak panelling brought originally from Hacking Hall, Darcy Lever, which was demolished in 1927. This panelling dates from 1640. In the Withdrawing-Room is an old carved settle. Yes, Hall-i' th'-Wood is an interesting place and has a picturesque appearance from the outside.

HEATON HALL

A Georgian Mansion, surrounded by its own park of about 600 acres, Heaton Hall stands four miles to the north of Manchester, amidst beautiful rose and old-fashioned flower gardens which in Spring and Summer-time make a delightful picture. A golf course; boating-lake, and surprisingly enough a reservoir, all take their part at Heaton.

This Hall, which was formerly the seat of the Egerton family, who became Earls of Wilton, was built in 1772, by Sir Thomas Egerton, the seventh baronet of a Cheshire family, which dates as far back as the Plantagenets. James Wyatt* the architect was commissioned to design it when quite a young man.

* James Wyatt was a brilliant architect. The sixth son of a timber-merchant in Stafford. In 1760 he went to Rome where he studied for five years. In 1766 he returned to London where after a short time he created a sensation in designing the Pantheon in Oxford Street, London, (a centre for concerts etc.). The drawings were exhibited at the Royal Academy, and in 1770 Wyatt was elected an Associate. He became exceedingly popular and one of his first commissions was the design for Heaton Hall. Buildings of his creation in the Classical and Renaissance style, include the Radcliffe Observatory, Oxford; The Canterbury Quadrangle at Christ Church, and the Library at Oriel College.

In 1796 James Wyatt was appointed Surveyor General to the Office of Works, and was engaged in improving Royal Palaces, including Windsor Castle.

James Wyatt was also made the Royal Academy's first Architect President.

HOLKER HALL.

HURSTWOOD HALL.

HULME HALL.

In Tudor times, one of the family was a Lord Chancellor, and ancestor of the Dukes of Bridge-water.

During the reign of James I Sir Roland Egerton was head of the family. His wife was a daughter of Lord Grey de Wilton, who had been Governor of Ireland during Elizabeth Is reign. He was made a baronet in 1617, and died in 1646, leaving estates in Cheshire, Staffordshire, and Northamptonshire.

During the reign of James I Richard Holland had taken up residence at Heaton in a house known as the Old Hall. He was succeeded by his brother's son, who was a Colonel under Cromwell, and in 1642 helped in the defence of Manchester. He was also a Member of Cromwell's Parliaments. In 1661, this Holland's brother succeeded. His daughter Elizabeth inherited both Denton and Heaton estates when her brother Edward died in 1683. Sir John Egerton, the third baronet, in 1684 married Elizabeth Holland of Denton and Heaton. Denton was a western Manor in the ancient Parish of Manchester, which the Hollands had owned since the fourteenth century. This had an estate of 35,000 acres.

Holland, the son of Elizabeth and Sir John Egerton, the third baronet, inherited as fourth baronet. He was a well-known antiquary. Holland's elder son died in 1744, aged twenty-five. The younger son Sir Thomas, the sixth baronet, was the Sir Thomas who in 1750 had built another house on the site of Heaton Hall, with a seven-window front, part of which still exists in the present building.

The next in succession, at the early age of seven, was Sir Thomas Egerton, the seventh baronet. In 1772 he became Member of Parliament for Lancashire. This was the time when at the age of twenty-three, he engaged James Wyatt to design the present Hall. The north side was left as it was but the brickwork covered with plaster and painted. A stone portico was also added. The building was extended to east and west by plastered wings with stone pilasters, and a new south front of yellow sandstone added projecting beyond the old one.

In 1784, Sir Thomas Egerton, the seventh baronet, was created Baron Grey de Wilton, and in 1801, became the Earl of Wilton. His only daughter was married to Lord Belgrave, who later became the first Marquess of Westminster. In 1814, their second son, Thomas, (born 1799), succeeded his grandfather. He married the Lady Mary Stanley, daughter of the twelfth Earl of Derby and his second wife Eliza Farren, an actress.

Charles Kemble's daughter Frances Anne, who was Mrs Siddon's niece, and an actress herself, visited Heaton Hall in 1830, meeting the second Earl of Wilton, who lived until 1882. His eldest son inherited only for three years, when his brother succeeded until 1896. In 1901, his son Arthur, the fifth Earl of Wilton, sold Heaton Hall, and Park, to the Manchester Corporation.

The beauty of these grounds owes much to the Civic authorities who created the lake and had the colonnade erected in 1912. This was part of the façade of the old Manchester Town Hall, in King Street, which was dismantled, and was designed by Francis Goodwin in the nineteenth century. The Temple once served as a summer-house for the Wilton family.

The Entrance Hall although small, is very charming, with plaster statues set in niches at semi-circular ends. The plaster decoration is of the Doric order. A very impressive feature is the Grand Staircase with its wrought iron handrail and beautiful tripods. The steps are of stone.

There is a wonderful two manual organ in the Music Room, which was made by Samuel Green, organ builder to George III. This is dated 1790. The full compass swell organ is thought to be unique at this date. (Public recitals are arranged.) Here the furniture is Chippendale, and there is a magnificent Bristol Glass Chandelier.

The Billiard Room ceiling has an attractive oval design in which a tazza-shaped urn is the main motive. This is repeated in the frieze above the chimney piece.

The Dining Room south wall has a semi-circular recess, probably originally made to hold a sideboard. Three painted panels take their place in the ceiling of the plasterwork. Here as in the Billiard Room are Venetian windows.

Up the Grand Staircase on to the first floor one can enter the Cupola Room, which is a striking and well-preserved example of the so-called Etruscan type of decoration, being a blending of the Raphael style with actual Roman motifs, and with subjects taken from vases thought to be Etruscan, and later discovered Greek. This work was carried out by Biagio Rebecca, the Italian who was associated with Wyatt. Only two or three other Etruscan Rooms survive in Great Britain.

The paintings at Heaton Hall were specially selected from the City's collection and are in keeping with the Georgian Period. Works include: a portrait of Sir Thomas Egerton, later first Earl of Wilton, as an archer, with Heaton Hall in the background, artist James Smith, 1783, Heaton Park Races, early nineteenth century, by F. C. Turner. Engravings which all come from the Frederick Behrens collection (gifted 1945). And also on view are Dutch paintings, and English silver lent by Mrs E. Assheton-Bennett,† English glass, also in the Assheton-Bennett collection in the ground floor Exhibition Gallery. In the small Dining Room and Library the furniture is Hepplewhite and Sheraton.

Heaton Hall has the distinction of being one of four Manchester buildings included in the very select group I of the Ministry of Town and Country Planning's Provisional list of buildings of special architectural or Historical interest. So the people of Manchester are fortunate in having such a place within easy reach, set in its own beautiful park.

HESKIN HALL

HESKIN HALL, which stands just outside Eccleston, Near Chorley, in seven and a half acres of land, is an Elizabethan manor house. It was previously owned by Lord Lilford, a former tyre salesman,

† Mr Edgar Assheton-Bennett, a wealthy Manchester-born stockbroker, died in 1964, and his widow Mrs Effie Assheton-Bennett, handed his magnificent art collection to the City, whose property it may eventually become. This very great treasure consists of one of the finest collections of Dutch and Flemish paintings in the world—97 paintings, and 323 pieces of seventeenth and eighteenth century English silver, the total value being about £2M. This collection is to be re-housed in the City Art Gallery, Mosley Street, Manchester.

HOPWOOD HALL.

HOUGH HALL.

whose ancestral home was Bank Hall, Bretherton. He still owns estates in the area but spends a great deal of time abroad. Lord Lilford is a Roman Catholic peer. His fourth wife Lady Lilford was a cabaret star. They were married in 1961. She completely modernized and refurnished the ten bedroomed Hall, which has an open-air swimming pool and miniature putting green.

The marriage failed and they were divorced in 1969, and Lady Lilford became the owner of the house which was included in a generous settlement. It is however to be sold, and expected to bring over £60,000, after which Lady Lilford hopes to live abroad with her four children, two of them being of a previous marriage to Nigel Spottiswoode, publisher. So Heskin Hall changes hands in 1969.

HEYWOOD HALL

IT may not be generally known even in Lancashire, that one of the main contributors implicated in the gunpowder treason was Peter Heywood. Yet this *was* so: for Heywood Hall, built during the sixteenth century was the birthplace, and country residence of the zealous Lancashire magistrate, Peter Heywood, of whom an account is given in Lord Clarendon's 'History of the Great Rebellion'.

It is said that he apprehended Guido Faux coming forth from the vault of the House of Parliament, on the eve of the gunpowder treason, November 5th, 1605.

He probably accompanied Sir Thomas Knevett, in his search of the cellars under the Parliament House. Mr Heywood narrowly escaped assassination at a subsequent period, by the hand of a Dominican friar, for urging 'poor Catholics' to take the oath of allegiance and supremacy. The renowned historian Stove, thus writes: 'In the late built Church of St Ann's, Aldersgate Street, London, is one flat stone in the chancel laid over Peter Heiwood, that deceased Nov. 2 1701, youngest son of Peter Heiwood, one of the Councillors of Jamaica, by Grace, daughter of Sir John Muddeford, Knight and Bart., great grandson of Peter Heiwood of Heiwood, in the County Palatine of Lancaster, who apprehended Guy Fawkes with his dark lanthorn, and for his prosecution of the Papists, as Justice of the Peace; was stabbed in Westminster Hall, by John James, Dominican Friar, Ann. Dom. 1640

'Reader! if not a Papist bred,
Upon such ashes lightly tread.'

HOGHTON TOWER

HOGHTON TOWER, Preston, is an early sixteenth century manorial House surrounded by a large park with oak woods, and from its position on a steep precipice about 560 feet above sea level, commands an interesting and wonderful view of the Fylde, Lake District, and even as far as the Welsh mountains.

The word Hoghton originates from an old English 'hoh' which means the spur or heel of a hill. The manor of Hoghton formed part of land which was given by the Conqueror to Roger de Poictou, who was first Lord of the Manor of Bolton. This great baron of Lancashire ranked amongst the Capitales Barones. He held 398 Manors under the Crown and all were confiscated. His title was Earl of Lancaster. In 1100 he was banished from England for taking part in the rebellion against Henry I. The De Hoghton family are traced back as far as this sovereign's time, to Hervey Walter, from whom descended Hervey Walter who had five sons, the successor being Hamo Pincerna, who married the daughter of Warin Bussel through whom he received the manor of Hoghton as a jointure. He died circa 1150. Warin Bussel was Baron of Penwortham. Next came William (1140) whose brother Ricardus Filius Harmonis Pincerna, living in 1189, seems to have succeeded him. The son of Richard was Adam, who in the reign of Henry II styled himself Adam de Hocton, or Adam Dominicus de Hocton. He held land in Hoghton in 1203, when it is thought a Pele tower may have been built. From him descended Adam, who had a son also named Adam, from whom descended Sir Adam de Hoghton Kt. His son Sir Richard succeeded in 1298 and died 1316-18. *His* son Sir Richard followed. He married Sibilla, heiress of the family De Iea (and a descendant of Earl Leofric and his wife Lady Godiva), in 1309, when she was aged thirty-six. Their son Adam de Hoghton inherited. He married twice, and was Knight of the Shire in 1349.

Next we have Sir Richard de Hoghton, Knight of the Shire in 1383, who founded a Chantry at Ribchester in 1406. John of Gaunt, King of Castile and Leon, Duke of Lancaster, in 1386 granted Sir Richard de Hoghton Kt., licence to enlarge his park. His son Sir William succeeded, then Sir Richard who died 1468. Sir Henry, who founded a Chantry in Preston Parish Church, died 1479. To Sir Alexander de Hoghton who was created knight banneret during the Scottish expedition of 1482, at the age of nineteen. His brother William succeeded. He married Margaret, daughter of Sir Chris. Southworth of Samlesbury, Kt. They had a son Richard who died 1559. He married four times.

The Rt Worshipful Thomas Hoghton succeeded his father, in 1558, at the age of forty-one. He was married to Catherine, daughter of Sir Thomas Gerard of Bryn. This Thomas was reputed to have built Hoghton Tower. A friend of Cardinal Allen he went into exile for religious reasons where he died in 1580. His son Thomas also went into exile and was ordained a Priest. On returning to Lancashire he was arrested and put in Salford jail where he probably died. His father's brother Alexander succeeded for about a year. Then his brother Thomas, whose son Sir Richard Hoghton during a glorious August in 1617 entertained King James I when he travelled from Scotland to London and stayed for three days, during which time he was said to have knighted the 'Sir Loin', in the Banqueting Hall. Many distinguished noblemen came to pay honour to His Majesty, and wearing the livery of their host Sir Richard were the tenantry and many families, making a splendid spectacle for the great occasion. His Majesty, dressed in his favourite colour 'green' with a feather in his cap and horn at his side presented a gay figure. The wine flowed and everyone was happy on this momentous visit. There was rush-bearing and the King went stag-hunting. The local people chose the time of the Royal visit to raise a petition for the return of Sunday pastimes which were previously prohibited by the puritans, with the result that His Majesty decreed that archery, ale-drinking, leaping, vaulting, and may-

KERSAL CELL. As John Byrom knew it.

KERSAL CELL. As we know it today.

poles should be allowed, but excluded bull-baiting and bowls.

The mother of the poet John Milton was said to have been descended from the de Hoghtons but there was some doubt about this.

In 1666 there were seventy-seven hearths taxed in the township and twenty-two of them were at Hoghton Tower.

Sir Gilbert Hoghton, son of Sir Richard succeeded. Born in 1591, he was also a favourite at the Court of James I. He was knighted in 1606 at the age of fifteen. He married Margaret, one of four daughters co-heiresses of Sir Roger Aston, Knt., of Cranford, Middlesex. Sir Gilbert was M.P. for Lancashire from 1614 to 1623, and High Sheriff in 1643. He died in 1645. Lady Margaret survived him twelve years.

Sir Richard Hoghton succeeded as third baronet. He married Sarah, daughter of Philip, Earl of Chesterfield. He was Knight of the Shire in 1656.

Sir Richard had lost four sons and the title fell onto his fifth son Charles, who was born in 1643. The fourth baronet was a scholar and mathematician. He built part of the Hoghton Tower on south side of lower courtyard—a three storied part, and was presumed to have employed Barnard Towneley, of Hurstwood, but this was not confirmed—the corbelled chimney stacks which he was famous for are at both Halls. Sir Charles died in 1710. His second son Sir Henry Hoghton, the fifth baronet, took part in the Jacobite rebellions, was J.P. and represented Preston in Parliament. Married three times, and died in 1768 aged ninety. Having no children the title passed to his brother's son.

Sir Henry Hoghton, sixth baronet, represented Preston in five Parliaments, and was leader of the Nonconformist Party.

The next in line of succession was Sir Henry Philip Hoghton the seventh baronet, born 1768. He succeeded in 1795. Was Colonel of the 3rd Royal Lancashire Militia from 1797 to 1803, died 1835.

In 1807 Hoghton Tower was in a disused condition except for the later built parts which were tenanted by a few families of weavers. There was much rotting and oak beams were reported to be hanging and plaster falling. However, Charles Dickens visited it in 1854 and afterwards made it the background for his short story entitled 'George Silverman's Explanation', so it couldn't be unfit to live in.

Sir Henry Philip Hoghton started restoring the building, his brother Charles continued with the job, and by 1901 it was completed by Sir James de Hoghton when the architect was Mr R. D. Oliver, of London.

Sir Henry Bold Hoghton the eighth baronet, married Dorothea, second daughter of Peter Patten Bold of Bold Esq., by whom he had five children.

A keen sportsman if one can call cock-fighting 'sport', and an enthusiastic yachtsman in the Royal Yacht Squadron, and with his famous schooner *Gypsy Queen* was a popular figure, but unlike another present day 'Gypsy' Sir Francis Chichester's *Gypsy Moth*, Sir Henry didn't always ride on the crest of a wave, and once ran high and dry on a sandbank near the Isle of Wight. Nevertheless she was famous in 1851. Sir Henry was High Sheriff of Lancashire in 1829.

The ninth baronet was also a Sir Henry. Born in 1821, he married three times, was educated at Harrow and St John's College, Cambridge. Was a magistrate and Deputy Lieutenant for Lancashire, and for Cardiganshire where he was High Sheriff. He sold Bold Hall in 1858, to a William Whitacre Tipping of Wigan, and in improving the Hoghton estate spent over £30,000 on drainage alone. In restoring much of the Hall he employed Messrs Paley & Austen of Lancaster. He died in 1876 and was buried at Farnworth. His brother Charles succeeded him. He was born in 1823, was a Captain of the 73rd Foot and later Adjutant of the 4th Lancashire Militia. Sir Charles was a Lay Rector of Preston, and highly esteemed for his kindly abstemious way of living.

And now we have Sir James de Hoghton, the eleventh baronet, C.B.E., and a J.P., and Deputy Lieutenant for Lancashire, Hon. Colonel and County Commandant of the Lancashire Volunteer Corps.

Sir James de Hoghton in 1901 completed restoring Hoghton Tower employing architect Mr R. D. Oliver of London. He was awarded the gold and silver medals of the Royal Humane Society for saving a James Dorling (who fell overboard from a yacht, from drowning).

In 1913 King George V and Queen Mary, visited Hoghton Tower during their state visit to Lancashire. A memorable occasion, the half-mile drive was lined with cheering people, and at the entrance to the Lower Courtyard they were greeted by Sir James and Lady de Hoghton, who were presented by Lord Derby. Sir James died in 1938. Sir Cuthbert de Hoghton, the twelfth baronet (born 1880), J.P. Lancashire, was educated at Harrow, and Magdelen College, Oxford. Was a Lieutenant in the Coldstream Guards, served in R.N.V.R., and R.N.A.S., in England and France during 1914-18 world war.

In 1917 he married his first wife Helen, daughter of Major Duncan MacDonald of Glencoe.

Sir Henry Philip Anthony Mary, de Hoghton, Bart, born on April 19th 1919, the eldest son of Sir Cuthbert de Hoghton, succeeded his father as the thirteenth baronet, of this great family.

Hoghton Tower, as previously stated, was built by the Right Worshipful Thomas Hoghton during the reign of Queen Elizabeth I about 1565, from local grit-stone taken from the quarry in the park. Roofs are of stone slates, gables covered with stone copings on the springers and apexes, on which are about fifty massive stone balls. Over the archway in the upper courtyard is a shield of arms bearing Thomas Hoghton's initials with date 1665. A leaden statue of William III which was taken from Walton Hall about 1834 when demolished stands in the inner courtyard. Having three towers the building is of imposing appearance and under the central tower is an entrance gateway under a depressed arch 12 feet wide with moulded capitals. Unfortunately the fine tower over the archway leading into the inner courtyard, was destroyed during the Civil Wars, when after the fall of Preston, Captain Starkey, of Blackburn, and one-hundred men were sent by the army of the Parliament to take Hoghton Tower. They were instructed to enter the gatehouse on an understanding that it should be surrendered upon quarter, but as soon as the Captain and men reached the upper rooms of the Tower it was blown up by gun-powder and all perished.

The Great Hall measures 54 feet long and 25 feet 9 inches wide and has a high flat ceiling divided by five beams boarded throughout, and ornamented with a geometrical pattern of moulded ribs, and oak panelled walls, with a flagged floor. It also has tran-

KNOWSLEY HALL.

somed windows and gabled bay on south side with fourteen light mullioned windows. The State Rooms were occupied by King James I during his stay in 1617, here we have the truly magnificent King's Hall measuring 38 feet by 20 feet. There is also a Billiard Room and Library. The Jacobean Stairway leads to the King's Room on upper floor north and Drawing-Room south. The King's Bedroom adjoins the north angle of the Tower.

In the S.E. Wing is another suite of stately rooms thought to have been used by the Duke of Buckingham during James Is visit.

About 1870 many valuable family paintings etc. were lost when they were placed in a pantechnicon after being previously stored away in London. When ready to be returned, a fire started in the vehicle and all were burnt to ashes. There are however still many treasures at Hoghton Tower, both in its collection and in its people. The family motto is 'Malgre le Tort'.

* With grateful acknowledgements to Mr Geo. C. Miller, from whose book 'Hoghton Tower' much information has been obtained for this chapter. (Published by the Guardian Press, Fishergate, Preston.)

HOLKER HALL

IT would be difficult to find a stately home in Lancashire more magnificent than Holker Hall, but as each has its own particular beauty and interests, comparisons are unnecessary and unfair, for after all an Englishman's home is his Castle, and what appeals to one person may not appeal to another, therefore I treat each in its own right, individually, and without prejudice.

This impressive House at Cark-in-Cartmel, Grange-Over-Sands, is surrounded by attractive gardens and parkland, where fallow deer have roamed freely for over two-hundred years. In Spring and Summer-time rhododendrons and many other flowers are a mass of colour and very beautiful.

Three families have in turn owned Holker: Prestons, Lowthers, and Cavendish's who are the present owners.

Richard Preston, was a Prior at Cartmel at the dissolution in 1536, and the Prestons acquired the land about 1556. George Preston built extensions onto the original old farm house known as Holker. In 1640, his son Thomas succeeded, who was followed by *his* son, another Thomas, who died in 1697, and was the last in the male line of the Prestons. Catherine Preston inherited from her father in 1697, she was married to Sir William Lowther, of Marske, in Yorkshire.

Holker Hall remained in the Lowther family's possession until 1756, since that date this beautiful Hall has belonged to the Cavendish family.

Catherine and Sir William Lowther had a son who succeeded as Sir Thomas, he married Lady Elizabeth Cavendish, daughter of the second Duke of Devonshire. Their son William died childless in 1756, at the age of twenty-nine, while at Holker, which passed to his cousin Lord George Augustus Cavendish, who was the nephew of his mother Lady Elizabeth (nee Cavendish). Lord George was the second son of the 3rd Duke of Devonshire. (His portrait can be seen in the Dining Room.) A Member of Parliament for fifty-six years he became Father of the House of Commons earning the name of 'Truth and Daylight'. A worthy name for a worthy Gentleman.

In 1871 whilst Lord Cavendish the seventh Duke of Devonshire owned Holker, a terrible fire destroyed the south-west wing completely, and many family treasures were lost including valuable paintings, a Canaletto and a Ruysdael among them. Lord Frederick Cavendish the seventh Duke of Devonshire rebuilt the wing, employing architects 'Paley and Austin' of Lancaster. The timber was used from the estate trees. This took three years to complete.

The old wing of this Hall is sixteenth/seventeenth century, and the new wing Victorian, of red sandstone, and like Queen Victoria herself has great dignity.

The seventh Duke, brought 3,500 volumes from Chatsworth for the Library. Some are books by the scientist Henry Cavendish (1731-1810), a grandson of the second Duke of Devonshire whom the Cavendish Laboratory at Cambridge is named after. In the Library and adjoining rooms is some very fine linenfold oak panelling.

The seventh Duke's second son Lord Frederick was killed in 1882 at Phoenix Park, Dublin. He had only just arrived to take up an appointment as Chief Secretary for Ireland when he and his Under-Secretary were stabbed to death. In the Library hangs his portrait, and one of his lovely wife Lady Frederick, who before marriage was Miss Lucy Lyttelton, one-time Maid-of-Honour to Queen Victoria, and a niece of Gladstone. Lady Frederick was also great-aunt of the Hon. Humphrey Lyttelton the Jazz Band leader. Here are many family portraits, including an outstanding drawing by John Sargent 1905, (which stands on an easel), depicting the present owner's mother, Lady Moyra Cavendish (nee de Vere Beauclerk) daughter of the tenth Duke of St Albans. There are also paintings of James I, Charles II, Oliver Cromwell and others. Two French Louis XVI, writing tables and a candelabra of the Regency Period, and a French ormolu clock of about two-hundred years old also add to the treasures. The fireplaces are of Derbyshire alabaster, inlaid with Italian marble.

Entering the Drawing Room which is rich and luxurious, it is obvious that Holker Hall is a much-loved home. The walls are covered with what is believed to be Macclesfield silk, dating from 1874. Here are more paintings by: Rhysdael, Gasper Poussin, Jean Baptiste and other masters, also portraits of the present members of the family. The fireplace here is of Carrara marble and a beautiful example of carving. A French tortoiseshell and ivory clock by Bains is dated 1740. Settees and chairs are of Hepplewhite design (c. late eighteenth century) and loose chintz covers of William Morris design. The signed photographs of King Alphonso and Queen Ena of Spain were presented to the father of Mrs Cavendish, Mr Hugh Lloyde Thomas, who was a member of the British Embassy in Madrid (1923). A Chippendale fretted gallery silver table holds a book on Buckingham Palace which was presented by Queen Mary to Lord Richard Cavendish (the present owner's father) to commemorate her visit to Holker Hall in 1937. Also to be seen is an embroidered face screen panel of Chinese symbols, worked by Mary Queen of Scots, while imprisoned at Old Chatsworth, and a collection of French fans which are all over two-hundred years old.

The Billiard Room has more fine paintings, including a well-known caricature by Sir Joshua Reynolds. There are two of Old Whitehaven, with whom the

KNOWSLEY HALL. From old Prints.

KNOWSLEY HALL.

41

Lowthers were very closely associated.

In the Dining Room is a Van Dyke self-portrait, also one of the present owner's grandfather Lord Edward Cavendish, who was the youngest son of the second Duke of Devonshire. And a portrait of Victor, aged nine years, who succeeded his uncle Spencer Crompton, Marquis of Hartingden, as the ninth Duke, while living at Holker. Spencer Crompton was a leading figure in political life, and declined the Premiership three times. Victor's rise to Dukedom brought courtesy titles to his younger brothers John, and *Richard*—who inherited Holker, and whose son Richard Cavendish is the present owner. As courtesy titles are not hereditary the present Richard Cavendish does not bear one.

Lady Dorothy MacMillan, daughter of Victor, the ninth Duke, was born at Holker.

Here the imposing fireplace was made from wood grown on the estate, and like all the other beautiful wood throughout this new wing, carved by local craftsmen. The four twisted pillars are very similar in style to those found in the old wing at Holker, Chatsworth House—the seat of the Dukes of Devonshire, and Cartmel Priory.

A large Spanish Chest made of Yew, could tell quite a story. This dates from the sixteenth century. The story goes that owing to their weight these chests were used for treasure at the time of the Armada. If the ship sank so would the treasure, keeping it safe from the enemy. Father Neptune must have oceans of jewels as well as pearls in his vast treasure trove—the sea.

At the foot of the staircase are portraits of Charles II and his wife Catherine of Braganza. The Venetian chandeliers are truly exquisite. They were believed to have been brought from Devonshire House, Piccadilly, London, when it was dismantled in 1920. Here near the window is a Chinese earthenware bath of over one-thousand years old. In old China these were kept in the courtyard and a fire lit underneath to heat the water. Fuel and water being scarce in those days, the ritual was that having heated the water sufficiently, all the family availed themselves of the same water, thus conserving both water and heat. On a marble topped Italian sidetable stands a most beautiful miniature pearwood carving of Leonardo da Vinci's 'Last Supper', Tyrolean, this is one-hundred years old.

The oak cantilever staircase in the Main Hall is unique, having over one-hundred balusters, each bearing a different design. This took three years to build.

The window on the landing is most interesting, bearing heraldic designs with the monograms and coronet of the seventh Duke, and coats of arms of the Clifford, Cavendish-Howard, Cavendish and Lowther families. The snake, which is the family emblem, is also depicted. And the motto 'Cavendo Tutus' . . . Translated this means 'Safety Through Caution', or proverbially 'Look Before you Leap'.

In the Wedgewood Bedroom is a four-poster bed by Hepplewhite, and in the Dressing Room can be seen some wonderful Wedgewood Jaspar pottery in pale blue, and early gentian etc. Here are some beautiful Gainsborough drawings. More Gainsborough work hangs in Queen Mary's Bedroom, so-named because Queen Mary used it during her visit in 1937. The oak tester bed has a lovely embroidered quilt worked by the Hon. Mrs Campbell Gray, the present owner's sister. All Holker Hall windows present a delightful view especially this one.

In the Dressing Room adjoining this bedroom the fire of 1871 began. It had spread into the Duke's Bedroom where scorch-marks still remain on the carpet. The pictures here must be mentioned: one a full-length photograph of the seventh Duke himself, dressed in the robes of Chancellor of the University of Cambridge; The Lady Moyra Cavendish, painted by Ross; and the Countess of Burlington, Lady Blanche, wife of the seventh Duke.

The Gloucester Bedroom and Dressing Room were used by the Duke and Duchess of Gloucester when they visited Holker in 1939. This bedroom contains some wonderful needlework in the nature of two sets of curtains, bed curtains and canopy, also bed-quilt all worked in the Jacobean style on Twill, and believed to be the work of Lady Moyra Cavendish.

The Gallery, contains several cabinets displaying some magnificent china, ivory, and other interesting items.

In the garden is an Historic Monkey Puzzle, Chilean tree, one of four planted in England by Joseph Paxton, landscape gardener to the sixth Duke of Devonshire. This is the sole survivor. It once blew down during a violent storm, but was saved by seven shire horses pulling it up with chains to its former position.

For thirsty visitors who are speechless after seeing so many wonderful things, a café is available on the premises. How nice to tell friends we have dined at the Hall, and even been inside Queen Mary's Bedroom.

This great family have reason to be proud of such an inheritance. Long may they live in their magnificent ancestral home, Holker Hall.

HURSTWOOD HALL

ABOUT one mile S.E. of Worsthorne, Burnley, in the small village of Hurstwood where Edmund Spenser the poet and writer of 'The Faerie Queen' found much of his inspiration, is the private residence of Mr and Mrs Kenneth Fielding, Hurstwood Hall, which was originally built in 1579, by Barnard Townley for he and his wife Agnes who was only ten years old when married. Their names together with the date are carved in large characters on a marriage plate over the front doorway as follows:

BARNARDUS TOWNLEY ET AGNES
EXOR EJUS 1579.

Barnard Townley was the son of John Townley, who was the third son of Sir Richard Townley of Townley. Barnard, an architect, was responsible for building part of Hoghton Tower. And was Clerk of Works to Sir Christopher Wren at the building of St Paul's Cathedral, London.

Agnes was the daughter and co-heiress of George Ormerod, of Ormerod, Gent, who died in 1602. John Townley, Gent, son of Agnes and Barnard Townley, died in 1704, leaving two daughters co-heiresses of whom Katherine, who was living in 1743, conveyed Hurstwood and Dunnockshaw to her husband Richard Whyte Esq., Deputy Governor of the Tower of London, who devised Hurstwood Hall to come to his nephew Richard Chamberlain, from whom it passed after an immediate descent by purchase in 1803 to Charles Townley of Townley Esq.

Some time ago the Hall was allowed to fall into a

LEIGHTON HALL.
Photograph
'Country Life'.

LEIGHTON HALL.
Photograph
'Country Life'.

very bad state of repair and was split up into three cottages and a shop, the rent of a cottage being one-shilling and tenpence a week, and the shop two-shillings and ten-pence.

Later George Thursby bequeathed Hurstwood Hall to his great-niece Miss Patience Anne Aspinall—during the last war, who decided to have the Hall restored to a Manor House and employed George Robb, the Manchester architect. The work started in 1961, taking four years to complete. The whole roof was re-slated, built up windows were restored, and the interior structure re-modelled. Plastering was removed from the walls revealing the original faced stonework, and oak beams were restored. Central-heating was also installed. Modern in some ways, especially the kitchen, yet Hurstwood Hall remains a superb example of an old Manor House with mullioned windows and stone walls etc.

There is a glorious view from the terrace across the Pennines, and Pendle Hill, famous for the Lancashire Witches is clearly visible.

The charming Mr and Mrs Kenneth Fielding now hold the Hall on a long lease, and obviously love their surroundings both indoors and outside where they have spent many hours in the garden which they have recently landscaped. And so have created great beauty in this restful corner of the Lancashire countryside.

HOPWOOD HALL

HOPWOOD HALL stands on a grassy hillock in a small wooded valley through which a brook runs south to join the Irk at Middleton.

From this family seat the knights Hopwode de Hopwode ruled their estates of Hopwood, Birch, Stanycliffe and Thornham for many centuries. 'Hop' in old English meant a small enclosed valley, and 'wode' signified wood. The family name of Hopwode dates from the time when a middleton knight was granted the land.

Still partly mediaeval, this hall in Tudor days was a large quadrangular brick and timber house with no less than fourteen hearths. It also had a dove-cote, and a water mill. It was much altered and added to. And in Jacobean times was again improved upon, the stairs were replaced by a Jacobean style staircase behind the withdrawing room, and a beautiful oak fireplace added.

John Hopwood, (whose father had settled to live at Stanycliffe Hall). Married Elizabeth of Speke, in 1687. He had the house remodelled extensively. The Tudor panelling was removed from the oak room, and larger panels replaced them. Next to the oak room the old timber kitchen was pulled down, and the brick banqueting Hall was built, this was made into a Chapel.

John and Elizabeth had a son Edmund Hopwood. He built the original library in 1755, in the Georgian style with shallow curving wooden bay. He also built the French Windows on the ground floor.

The Gregge-Hopwoods took over the estate in 1773, and in 1840 Robert Gregge-Hopwood made great improvements. He turned the banqueting hall into a kind of Victorian drawing room, and had a dining room built to replace the corridor on the east side of the court. Countess Mary Augusta Sefton, (his daughter) planned the interior of this large room.

In 1855, the Hall was owned by Susan Fanny Gregge-Hopwood. A lover of antiques, she determined to restore the Jacobean and Tudor parts of the house, and also added period furniture and large vases.

In 1947, the Manor House of Hopwood Hall was acquired by the De la Salle Brothers for their teacher's College. So with evidence of building from fourteenth to the present century, the old Hall of Hopwood remains.

HOUGH HALL

THE originally black-and-white half-timbered building known as Hough Hall, off Moston Lane, Moston, has suffered the wear and tear of many other smaller halls. Built during the reign of Henry VIII by George Halgh, it remained the property of the Halgh's until 1678. The last of the family to live there was Robert Halgh who left the Hall and estate to his illegitimate son John Dawson who sold it to James Lightbowne, of the Lightbowne Hall family.

Later, Hough Hall passed to the Minshull family of Chorlton, one of whom was Elizabeth Minshull, who became the third wife of poet John Milton. Elizabeth was a cousin of Dr Paget, a minister of Blackley Chapel.

The next owner of this residence was Cornet Roger Aytoun, known to his fellow-dragoons as 'Spanking Roger'. Handsome and smart in more ways than one, he married in 1769, (at the Collegiate Church), Mrs Barbara Minshull, a widow, of Chorlton Hall. Her late husband, an apothecary, had left her quite a fortune. Barbara, many years Roger's senior, died fourteen years later, and within a year he married again. But this owner of Hough Hall and other properties after only one week with his new bride a Miss Sinclair, of Scotland, (his own native land), deserted her. Before his death in 1810, Roger Aytoun achieved high military rank.

Hough Hall, in a much neglected condition was then bought by Samuel Taylor, who had much property in Moston and Blackley. When he died the hall and land went to brothers Robert and John Ward, who having previously lived in a small cottage off Kenyon Lane, Moston, where they were born, had worked hard and built up a successful textile business in Manchester. So they took great pride and joy in owning the Hall, where Robert and his family lived. John became one of the first councillors and the first alderman when the district became incorporated in the city, in 1890.

Robert Ward died in 1904, and was buried in the family vault in Blackley Churchyard.

Hough Hall remained in the family for some time, but later passed into other hands, and was used as a doctor's surgery, and for other purposes—even for lipstick manufacture. Now, however, Hough Hall is no painted lady, indeed her once lovely black-and-white half-timbered walls are to put it politely—off-white, but then she has even been adapted as offices for a coal merchant. Her most precious jewels have changed to—black diamonds.

HULME HALL

HULME HALL, was formerly the seat of a branch of the Prestwich family. During the Civil Wars, Sir Thomas Prestwich being much impoverished, sold

ORDSALL HALL.

Painting, Margaret Chapman.

the Mansion and estate in 1660, to Sir Oswald Mosley.

Through his Mother he had advanced large sums of money to Charles I under the assurance that she had hidden treasure with which to repay him, either in the Hall or grounds. Time passed, and the old Lady Dowager was struck down with apoplexy before revealing to her son the treasure's whereabouts. After she died a search was made without result and he himself died in a state of poverty. The spells and demons were said to have guarded the treasure only too well.

The Hall passed into other hands and was eventually purchased by the Duke of Bridgewater. Much later it was pulled down but no treasure was revealed.

KERSAL CELL

KERSAL CELL, is a most interesting smaller building with quite a history, and is said to owe its origin to the grant of the 'Hamlet of Kersal' to monks of the Cluniac Priory, Lenton, Nr Nottingham, by Randle Gernons, Earl of Chester and Lord of South Lancashire. The building of a place for the service of God, being the object of the Earl's gift. A Cell was established soon afterwards, when Henry II regranted the 'Hermitage of Kersal' to the Priory, after resumption by the Crown in 1164 or 1176 of the Honour of Lancaster. Presumably dedicated to St Leonard, the Cell for about fifty years only housed two or three monks at a time.

During the fourteenth century French Wars, Kersal Cell was said to have been in the hands of the Crown, but several grants to Lenton Priory in 1392 saved it temporarily until final dissolution of the Abbey in 1539. The Kersal Property was then leased at a rent of £11.6.8d. to a John Wood for twenty-one years, after which it was sold for £155.6.8d. to Baldwin Willoughby, who in 1540 sold it to Ralph Kenyon, of Gorton, who re-sold two-thirds of the estate to James Chetham and Richard Siddall, of Slade Hall, retaining the Cell and Monastic buildings for himself, which remained with the Kenyon family until after the Restoration when Ralph Kenyon's great-grandson George transferred them to Edward Byrom of Manchester. So Kersal Cell became the well-loved home of the famous Jacobite, Hymn-writer, Poet, and Stenographer John Byrom who was born in 1691. His father, a linen draper, sent him to school at Chester, and later to an important London Public School 'Merchant Taylor's'. John made such remarkable progress and became a Fellow of Trinity College, Cambridge. (Interesting to note that while at College John wore a wig made from the locks of his sister.)

On returning to Kersal, John, known as a genial and spirited young man, used to stand on the banks of the River Irwell, not far from the Cell, every night and morning, reciting Tully's Oratories in Latin with a loud voice. His sister stated in a letter dated 4th October 1712, 'He bawls so loud they can hear him a mile off, so that all the neighbours think he is mad, and you would if you saw him'. She also added: 'Sometimes he thrashes corn with John Rigby's men, and helps to get potatoes, and works as hard as any of them.' and that he was very good company.

In 1717, John Byrom spent a year at Montpelier, in France, studying medicine, and in 1721, married his cousin, then became a teacher of shorthand, and was admitted into the Royal Society which enabled him

to rank among pupils: The Duke of Devonshire; Lord Chesterfield; Horace Walpole, and other noteables.

It was at Kersal Cell that in 1745 John composed the stirring Carol 'Christians Awake', presenting it to his daughter Dorothy as a Christmas gift, headed 'Christmas Day for Dolly', and in 1751 she heard it sung for the very first time from her position in an upper-room window, by choristers. How proud and delighted Dorothy must have felt.

Here John Byrom spent many hours in a dimly-lit room writing immortal works, and letters to friends John, and Charles Wesley (1707-1788) the composer of six-thousand hymns including 'Jesu, Lover of my Soul'. Also school-master friend John Clayton. Kersal Cell is said to be haunted by the ghost of a 'grey monk' but the spirit of John Byrom the great genius also seems to linger.

In August 1745, Byrom's eldest daughter Elizabeth or 'Beppy', kept a lively account in her diary of 'The Forty-five', of the main events of the Prince of Wales' march, and in August she accompanied her brother in North Lancashire on a tour, visiting Blackpool and Lytham for a gallop on the sands. On her return home in the middle of September, Miss Elizabeth stated 'There is already great talk of the Pretender coming'. Tradition says the young Chevalier paid John a secret visit at Kersal Cell, being lodged for the night. Well, there were secret hiding-places, and stumbling blocks to give warning of anyone approaching which made hiding easy. And a secret passage measuring about six feet high was discovered when part of the ground collapsed under a coal man's heavy lorry.

John Byrom died in 1763, and was buried in the Byrom Chapel at Manchester Cathedral. The Byrom line became extinct on the death of his great-granddaughter Miss Eleanora Atherton in 1870. Kersal Cell then passed to her God-son Edward Fox, who assumed the name of Byrom. Kersal 'Mill' (shown on the 1845 ordnance map) was pulled down many years ago. An old house known as Kersal 'Cottage' stood almost opposite this mill, probably the one on the 'fringe of the moor' to which George Kenyon, the third, retired with his family after the Cell was disposed of to the Byroms.

When the Manchester Whitsuntide horse races first started in 1730 on Kersal moor, much controversy arose as to whether they should be stopped or not. Ashton Lever and William Hulton advocated them, and were opposed by Edmund Chetham, Mr John Byrom, M.A., and Mrs Anne Chetham who succeeded in having them discontinued from 1745 to 1760, when they were resumed again.

Kersal Cell had north and south wings of brick added before 1850 by Miss Atherton. The old centre block being black-and-white half-timbered with gabled roofs, projecting oriels and mullioned windows. The east-end room, known as the 'Oak Parlour' was divided from the Refectory by a passage with a porch at the end leading into the front garden. One window of this room being particularly interesting shows a shield of three 'Battle-axes' with the name Aunesworth—said to be the family arms of Harrison Ainsworth who was known to have been a frequent visitor there. The passage dividing north and south wings of the house was called the 'Cloister'.

About thirty years ago there was some doubt as to the future of Kersal Cell, which stands about three miles north of Manchester, and about a quarter-of-a-

ORDSALL HALL, SALFORD.

ORDSALL HALL.
Old Print.

mile from the site of Kersal Hall which was completely demolished in 1936, and the now adopted by America Agecroft Hall. But during the second World War, Charles P. Hampson of 'Kersal Cell Preservation Committee' was in charge, and this ancient residence was saved from an undecided fate, and is still going strong, although not being used for its original purpose. Time has changed the scene, and the 'grey monk' has chance to become a 'Gay' monk, for the picturesque Kersal Cell is now a 'Country Club'.

KNOWSLEY HALL

KNOWSLEY HALL, is the stately home of the Stanley family, many generations having lived there in splendour.

The name 'Stanley' was derived from a hamlet in Leek, Staffordshire, known as Stony Lea. 'Stan' being Anglo-Saxon for stone, for the ground was noted for its stony quality. A Chapel of St Leonard once stood on the site—a dependency of Burscough Priory.

The Stanleys were a branch of the Staffordshire Audleys, said to have been Barons by tenure before the reign of Henry III. From them descended the Touchets, Barons Audley, Peers of the Realm. Of these Audleys was the Lord James, who gallantly broke through the French army at Poitiers, fighting until covered in blood, and after the victory was interviewed by the Black Prince.

The Audley family were probably founded during the reign of Henry I when one of the founder's grandsons William, being much attached to Stoney Lea, later, during the reign of King John, exchanged some other land for it with his uncle. From this William de Stanleigh (later converted into Stanley), descended the Stanleys of Hooton, Lathom, and Knowsley, Alderley and others. William married Jane, daughter and co-heiress of Sir Philip Bamville, of Storeton, Cheshire. The Stanleys then moved to Cheshire. A descendant of William's also named William de Stanley, married the heiress of Hooton, (which is a place half-way between Chester and Birkenhead). So the Stanleys of Storeton became the Stanleys of Hooton, who centuries later, after the restoration of Charles II, were raised to the baronetage.

From Sir John Stanley, younger brother of William of Hooton, sprang the Stanleys of Knowsley, Earls of Derby, and the Barons Stanley of Alderley.

In 1385, John, who was the second son of the Chief Forester of Wirral, married Isabel, daughter of Sir Thomas de Lathom, thus becoming owner of Lathom and of Knowsley. Richard II made him Lord Deputy of Ireland and gave him grants of land there. Later, under Henry IV he became Lord Lieutenant. The King transferred to him the Lordship of the Isle of Man. He was also Treasurer of the Royal Household. Henry V gave him the Garter. Sir John died in 1413. His grandson Thomas also became Lord Lieutenant of Ireland. He was summoned to Parliament as Lord Stanley in 1456, and so took place the rise of the Stanleys to the peerage; succeeded by his son Thomas, the second Lord Stanley, who in 1457 married Eleanor, daughter of Richard Neville, Earl of Salisbury, and sister of the Earl of Warwick, the most powerful noble of the day, known as the 'Kingmaker'. Lord Stanley was knighted in 1460 by Henry IV. Was Chief Justice of Chester P.C., and in 1485 was created first Earl of Derby.

In 1459 Civil War broke out afresh and that same year Warwick's father and Lord Stanley's father-in-law, the Earl of Salisbury, with five-thousand men, routed a force commanded by the King's friend Lord Audley (one of the Audleys from which the Stanleys originated) at Bloreheath, Staffordshire. After much fighting Warwick was slain on 14th April 1471. The following month the cause was overthrown, and on the 22nd of the same month Henry VI died a prisoner in the Tower. About three years later, Lord Stanley was appointed Steward of the Yorkist King's Household, a high and confidential office. In 1475, he accompanied Edward IV on the invasion of France. Seven years later, Richard, Duke of Gloucester, soon to become Richard III was sent on an expedition to Scotland. Lord Stanley commanded under him the right wing four-thousand strong of the invading army, they stormed Berwick-upon-Tweed, which remained English afterwards. Edward IV died in 1483. In 1485, Lord Stanley's action at Bosworth Field secured the throne for Henry VII. After the battle he was created Earl of Derby and was constituted one of the Commissioners for executing the office of Lord High Steward of England on the day of Henry VIIs Coronation. Lord Stanley had married twice; his second wife was Margaret Beaufort, Countess of Richmond. Her first husband being Edmund Tudor, Earl of Richmond, thus she became mother of Henry VII, Margaret was daughter and sole-heiress of John Beaufort Duke of Somerset, Henry VIIs Captain, and great-granddaughter of John of Gaunt. Her grandfather John, Earl of Somerset, was the son of John of Gaunt and Catherine Swynford. Margaret was aged forty when her second husband Sir Henry Stafford died, and by her marriage to the Earl of Derby, this great nobleman whom Edward IV delighted to honour became step-father to a King.

This first Earl of Derby was appointed 'Constable of England' for life from 1483. He was present at the funeral of Edward IV. His eldest son George, was married to Joanna, daughter and heiress of John, Lord Strange of Knockin, thus the title Lord Strange was for some time the courtesy title of the eldest sons of the Earls of Derby.

King Henry VII paid an official visit to Knowsley and Lathom Halls for which the Earl of Derby made great preparations, and built an extension onto Knowsley. This part of the building is called the 'Royal Lodging'. The King stayed a month, (Circa 1495).

Lord Derby died at Lathom in 1504, aged about seventy, and was buried at Burscough. Margaret (who was the founder of St John's and Christ's Colleges, Cambridge), died in 1509, the same year as her son, and was buried in Westminster Abbey.

Lord Derby's first wife the Lady Eleanor, had borne him six sons and four daughters. Only two of the sons survived him—Edward and James. Edward Stanley's second wife was daughter of Sir John Harrington, of Hornby, who with his father Sir Thomas, was committed to the custody of Lord Derby after the battle of Bloreheath. The King honoured him with a peerage after the battle of Flodden, and also proclaimed him Lord Monteagle, saying that his ancestors bore the crest with the eagle (Mount and Eagle). The Monteagle barony has long since died out.

The other surviving son James Stanley, succeeded his uncle James as Warden of Manchester, and rose to Bishop of Ely in 1506. *His* son James Stanley, of

ORDSALL HALL.
Interior of bay window of
Banqueting Hall.

PENNINGTON
HALL.

49

Harford, also distinguished himself at Flodden.

Thomas, the second Earl of Derby, grandson and heir of the first Earl, attended Henry VIII in the 1513 French expedition and fought at the Battle of the Spurs. He married Anne, sister of George, the first Earl of Huntingdon. His son Edward (1509-1572) the third Earl, was cup-bearer at Queen Anne Boleyn's Coronation on 31st May 1533, K.G. Bearer of the 'Curtana' at the Coronation of Edward VI P.C., Lord Lieutenant of Lancashire, and Lord High Steward and bearer of the 'Curtana' at Mary Ist's Coronation 1553, and Vice-Admiral of Chester and Lancashire etc. He married three times, and lived in great splendour and employed two-hundred persons including a Trumpeter, and a 'Fool'. This Earl was succeeded by his son by his first wife Dorothy, the daughter of Thomas Howard, second Duke of Norfolk. Edward, the third Earl died at Lathom House in 1572. His son Henry, succeeded as fourth Earl as previously mentioned. He was also one of the Commissioners for the trial of Mary Queen of Scots.

William Shakespeare is said to have visited Knowsley in 1589, as a member of Lord Essex's troupe of players, no doubt playing his part magnificently in this 'Hall of Kings'.

The fifth Earl, Ferdinando, (1559-1594) succeeded his father as Lord Lieutenant of Lancashire and Cheshire and Vice-Admiral. He married Alice, daughter of Sir John Spencer, of Althorpe. A tragic life, he rejected a treasonable project to assume the Crown in the right of his grandmother Mary, daughter of Henry VII and was thought to have been poisoned by the originators of the plot. This unfortunate Earl died at the early age of thirty-five. A poet of merit—who knows what heights he would have reached had he lived longer? Also buried at Ormskirk. There were three daughters of the marriage. Countess Alice re-married in 1600 becoming the third wife of Lord Chancellor Ellesmere, ancestor to the Duke of Marlborough.

William, the brother of Ferdinando, male heir, succeeded as sixth Earl when aged thirty-two and was also Lord Lieutenant and Vice-Admiral of Lancashire and Cheshire, and Admiral of the 'Isle of Man'. In 1594 he married Elizabeth, sister and co-heir of Henry, the eighth Earl of Oxford. Having made over the care of most of his estates to his son Lord Strange he lived privately at Bidston Hall, Wirral. He died in 1642, and was buried at Ormskirk.

James Stanley, the seventh Earl of Derby. (The 'Martyr Earl'), was born at Knowsley in 1607, exactly a year after Guy Fawkes was executed for the 'Gunpowder Plot'. His father was William, the sixth Earl, and his mother the eldest daughter of Edward Vere, the seventh Earl of Oxford. James Stanley was the eldest of three sons. In 1625, he was elected M.P. for Liverpool. A year later he married Charlotte, de la Tremouille, the daughter of Claude de la Tremouille, Duc de Thouars, a French Nobleman. Her mother was a daughter of William the Silent. The wedding took place in the Prince of Orange's Palace at the Hague, in the presence of the King and Queen of Bohemia.

The seventh Earl formed a 'Well-stocked' Library at Knowsley, including books of great volume and of lesser volume.

In 1628, the Lieutenancy of North Wales was bestowed on Lord Strange and he was summoned to the House of Lords as Sir James Stanley de Strange, Chevalier. He took his seat in the House of Peers in 1629, and became Earl of Derby in 1642. In the same year he joined Charles I at York.

In 1644, Lathom House was besieged, and surrendered to Parliament in 1645. During this time Lady Derby was exceedingly brave and a true heroine. Lord Derby secured the Isle of Man for the King, and fought at Marston Moor. His estates were confiscated. The Earl sent his wife to the Isle of Man where he also stayed at Rushen Castle for a while, but in 1651, left to join Charles II in the march from Scotland to England. Lord Derby was severely wounded at Wigan Lane, but later rejoined Charles at Worcester. While retreating to Lancashire from this defeat he was captured and imprisoned at Chester Castle.

James Stanley, the courageous seventh Earl of Derby, who hid King Charles II, at Boscobel, was unjustly executed at Bolton, on September 3rd 1651 and buried at Ormskirk.

In 1702, on the death of the ninth Earl, who was buried at Ormskirk, Lathom Hall passed by descent to his daughter Lady Ashburnam.

James, the tenth Earl, brother and heir of the ninth, was M.P. 1685-1702.

Knowsley Hall was almost completely rebuilt by the tenth Earl, the part which is of red brick with white stone dressings was his work. An art lover, he commissioned local artist Hamlet Winstanley to buy paintings for him on the continent. These are still part of the Knowsley collection.

The tenth Earl died in 1736, without male heir, and the Lordship of Man, and barony of Strange, with a large part of the estates, devolved upon the issue of his Aunt, whose grandson James, second Duke of Atholl, became heir general to the Martyr Earl. The Earldom of Derby together with Knowsley and other estates passed to the branch of the family who were baronets of Bickerstaffe. Edward Stanley, the fifth baronet became eleventh Earl of Derby in 1736. He was the son of Sir Thomas Stanley Bt., of Bickerstaffe. Born at Preston in 1689, was Mayor of Preston 1731-32. M.P. for Lancashire, and Chancellor of the Duchy of Lancaster. Sir Thomas Stanley Bt., died in 1776 aged eighty-seven, two days before his wife, and they were both buried at Ormskirk.

Edward, the twelfth Earl was the grandson of the eleventh Earl. Lord Lieutenant of Lancashire for fifty-eight years; twice Chancellor of the Duchy of Lancaster. A keen sportsman, he was founder of the 'Derby' and the 'Oaks', supported 'Cock-fighting', etc. His son Edward Smith inherited as thirteenth Earl. Knight of the Garter, Lord Lieutenant of Lancashire. Was created Baron Stanley of Bickerstaffe, in 1832. A noteable zoologist, intensely interested in Natural History—the aviaries, conservatories, animal sheds, are the result of this. His menagerie at Knowsley cost him about £10,000 a year, with 318 species of birds, 94 species of mammalia containing 345 individuals, and hundreds more rare creatures. This Earl was a friend of Edward Lear who wrote his famous 'Nonsense Songs and Stories' for the children of the house. The thirteenth Earl died in 1851, aged seventy-seven, and was buried at Ormskirk. He was succeeded by his son Edward Geoffrey the fourteenth Earl. M.P. for Stockbridge 1820-26, for Preston 1826-30, Windsor 1830-32, and for North Lancashire 1832-46. Prime Minister 1852, 1858-59 and 1866-68. Chief Secretary for Ireland 1830-33. Chancellor of Oxford University 1853, and Lord Rector of Glasgow 1834. A brilliant poet and orator, this great man died in 1869 aged seventy, and was buried at Knowsley. Edward Henry, the son of

PLATT HALL.

RADCLIFFE TOWER.

the fourteenth Earl, succeeded as the fifteenth Earl. He made many alterations in Knowsley Hall. The fifteenth Earl died in 1893.

His brother Frederick Arthur was the sixteenth Earl, and was succeeded by his eldest son Edward George Villiers. Both men were prominent in public life.

The seventeenth Earl rebuilt much of Knowsley Hall, added another storey to the main block, placing the family crest 'The Eagle and Child' on its summit in Portland Stone.

Edward John, the present and eighteenth Earl of Derby, was born in 1918. Grandson of the seventeenth Earl. Educated at Eton and Oxford. On the 22nd July 1948, married Lady Isabel Milles-Lade, daughter of Mrs Esther Milles-Lade and the late Hon. Henry Augustus Milles-Lade. Became Lord Lieutenant of the County Palatine of Lancaster in January 1951, but resigned in May 1968, to enable him to be more active in political and social life.

The Stanleys, Earls of Derby, have been, and will continue to be a very great family. Their Knowsley residence is a place of magnificence, but is no longer open to the public having been closed for over ten years.

The Large Library with its beautiful white and gold bookcases contains the exclusive Natural History Books. Here is a Chippendale Mirror of unbelievable beauty, reflecting the whole length of the room. In the over-mantel of the elaborate fireplace is a picture of the Cavalier Earl. There are also paintings by Nicholas and Gaspar Poussin.

The Stucco Room was built by the tenth Earl to link the Royal Apartments with the House proper, and is a ballroom where the original scheme of decoration still survives. Here Queen Elizabeth has dined.

The Porch leading into the Entrance Hall was built by the present Earl. Here inside are many fine paintings and late sixteenth or seventeenth century furniture. On either side of the entrance door is a pair of Queen Anne side-tables. The seventeenth century fire-dogs add their own particular charm.

Outside are gardens with spacious lawns and stately trees. There are lakes on which wild fowl love to glide. The Rose Gardens are very beautiful in the summertime, and the whole atmosphere is one of tranquillity. The Stanley Family Motto is 'Sans Changer'.

LEIGHTON HALL

LEIGHTON HALL, Carnforth, has the most superb setting. Surrounded by spacious fields, beautiful woodland park, and the full range of Lakeland Mountains at the back, this turreted castle-like building has an almost dream quality. The Gothic façade of sparkling white lime-stone believed to have been built in 1800, by Harrison of Chester, stands on the site of a much older House. The new wing was erected in 1870 'by Austin and Paley' of Lancaster.

The Entrance Hall, with its gracefully curved stone staircase and Gothic pillars is impressive. Here are seventeenth century chairs, a Louis XV bracket clock, paintings of horses, and one on the staircase by Copley Fielding, which is thought to be the largest picture he ever painted, also other fascinating treasures.

In the Dining Room, the windows are neo-Gothic, and picture panels of early eighteenth century Flem-ish. The silver candelabra of tree design was bought by Mr R. T. Gillow in 1851 at the Great Exhibition. There are also glass ones which he bought at the first Paris Exhibition in 1860. The exquisite glass pair on the mantelpiece are eighteenth century French.

On entering the Drawing Room one is immediately aware of a woman's touch there is such a friendly welcoming atmosphere. Here can be seen an early eighteenth century games table of Gillow design, on top of which is a small case containing a genuine lock of the hair of King James II set in gold, (a rare treasure indeed). This was given by Prince James Edward Stuart to Henry Fallowfield during the revolt of 1715. Henry Fallowfield's daughter married one of the Gillows and she is an ancestor of the present Mrs Reynolds.

An artistic family, the Miss Gillows left their mark in a set of beautifully embroidered chairs. Some paintings should be noted on these walls, among them being a bathing scene by Gaspar Poussin, and two by Guardi.

At Leighton Hall there is a real artist's studio, for Mrs Reynolds is a professional painter. One can see her personality reflected in most of the rooms, but this one outshines them all, with her own paintings, many of which are exhibited. More of Mrs Reynolds pictures can be seen in the State Bedroom which is a good example of the late-Victorian Period.

Major and Mrs Reynolds are also great music lovers, this is obvious in the Music Room, which was at one time a billiard room. There are various loud-speakers, a radio, and a Grand Piano. This was no doubt used to accompany the wonderful singer Kathleen Ferrier on her last performance at a Private House, and before a select audience.

The history of the family at Leighton Hall goes back many years when in 1246, Adam de Avranches had a fortified Manor there, the land having been granted to him in 1173, by William de Lancaster, Baron of Kendal. Adam's daughter Ellen married Adam de Redman, thus inheriting. Leighton Hall next went to his sister and heiress who married Adam de Yealand—Adam seems to have been a popular name in the family. The daughter of the last Adam, Alice, married Robert Conyers. Their daughter married William Croft of Dalton. The last of the Croft family was Nicholas. His daughter Alison, married Geoffrey Middleton, of Middleton-in-Lonsdale. He was followed by his son Robert, who married Ann. She was the last of the great crusading family of de Beetham, of Beetham Hall. Their son Thomas Middleton inherited. He married a Strickland of Sizergh, and died in 1518. Next came his son Gervase who was the owner of Leighton during the time of the Reformation. He was faithful to his religious beliefs, and during those disturbing days a Priest was hidden in the House. George Middleton, the son of Gervase came next, and from his Mrs Reynolds the present owner, descended through another family. Thomas followed, he married a de Hoghton, of Hoghton Tower. Their son George was a distinguished Cavalier and Colonel of the Royal Army in 1642. He was Knighted and made a Baronet at Durham. Twice High Sheriff of Lancashire, he paid £2,646 in fines during Cromwellian times through his loyalty to the Crown. He was succeeded by his grandson George Middleton Oldfield.

The next owner of Leighton Hall was Albert Hodgson, who was married to Dorothy, the daughter of George Middleton Oldfield. In the 1715 Rebellion

RADCLIFFE TOWER, GREAT HALL.

he was taken at Preston. Leighton was confiscated and in 1722 sold by auction when it was bought for Mr Hodgson by a friend Mr Winkley, of Preston. Albert Hodgson, after his release from prison, returned to Leighton which had been badly damaged and burned, and was heavily mortgaged. However, Mary, his daughter, married George Towneley of Towneley, who rebuilt the house in 1763. A plain classical house rather in the style of the Adams brothers. There were no children of the marriage. In 1784, Mr Towneley died, and his nephew John sold Leighton Hall in 1786, to Thomas Worswick of Ellel Grange, a banker, whose wife was Alice Gillow.

Thomas's son Alexander unfortunately failed in business after the Napoleonic Wars and in 1822 he sold the property to Richard Gillow, his cousin, and the grandson of the founder of the well-known furniture business 'Gillow and Co' of Lancaster. Much Gillow furniture can be seen at Leighton Hall, and lovely work it is. The family motto 'PERSEVERANDO' (By Perseverance) has brought perfection.

Richard retired from the business when he went to live at Leighton. He was married to a Stapleton of Carlton Towers, Yorkshire. Richard Thomas Gillow, their son, succeeded in 1849, and living until aged ninety-nine was known as the 'Old Squire'. In 1853, he built the Roman Catholic Church in Yealand, and in 1870, the new wing at Leighton Hall.

Richard Thomas Gillow died in 1906, and his grandson Charles Richard Gillow inherited, who died in 1923. His Widow died at Leighton in 1966 at the age of ninety-six, leaving still living at Leighton, her two daughters Mrs Reynolds and Miss Gillow, also Mr James R. Reynolds, her son-in-law, who is the son of the late Sir James P. Reynolds Bt., of Woolton, Nr Liverpool.

A very interesting family are the owners of fascinating Leighton Hall.

LYTHAM HALL

SITUATED in its beautiful parkland, Lytham Hall still stands supreme, although part of its grounds are invaded by other buildings, and the rooms used by a well-known assurance company.

In 1606, Cuthbert Clifton bought the manor of Lytham from Sir Richard Molyneux, and after pulling down an old priory he built a Mansion House. In 1617, Sir Cuthbert was knighted by James I at Lathom House. He had twelve children, two of whom were killed in the war. His son Thomas was a Royalist. The Cliftons were Roman Catholics and in 1694 Sir Thomas Clifton was unjustly accused of treason and imprisoned. He died at the age of sixty-six shortly after being acquitted. His nephew succeeded. Thomas Clifton of Fairsnape, whose grandson Thomas Clifton in 1757 built Lytham Hall, which was completed in 1764. The present Georgian Hall of hand-made brick with stone dressings was built on, or near the site of the previous hall, which was partially destroyed by fire, and existed until about Mid-eighteenth century. Part of the old building was joined with the new, and goes to form the two-storeyed wing and other parts. John Carr, of York designed this Hall, he was a noted architect of his day, and was the designer of Harewood House and other buildings of importance.

The interior with its spacious rooms has some interesting carved mantelpieces. Although no longer a private residence the home of the Clifton family is still serving a useful purpose.

ORDSALL HALL

GREEN fields and an avenue of stately trees were at one time the setting for Ordsall Hall, originally a quadrangular half-timbered building standing on the banks of the River Irwell, Salford. This Hall has long since lost its beautiful surroundings and defensive moat through the destructive and creative powers of man. Houses and factories now obstruct the view—the penalty of progress.

The De Ferrers, Earls of Derby, in the thirteenth century were Lords of the Manor, one of whom in 1225 gave Pendleton Manor to his estate agent Robert Hulton, who left the tenancy to a cousin David Hulton who later, in 1251, exchanged it for Ordsall. His eldest son Richard succeeded, who married Margery, daughter of Robert de Radcliffe, of Radcliffe Tower. Robert Radcliffe de Ordsall, was High Sheriff of Lancashire 1340-1341.

Sir John Radcliffe de Ordsall, Knight of the Shire, born about 1300, attended Edward III in France in 1345, and was given the family motto of: 'Caen, Crecy, Calais,' after battles in which he distinguished himself. Sir John married Lady Joan Holland, sister of the first husband of Joan, Countess of Kent (a widow) who married the Black Prince, thus connecting the Radcliffes with the Royal family.

In 1351, Ordsall Hall was a farmhouse which it remained for many years. Sir John, whose descendants owned Ordsall for the next three-hundred years, died in 1362. His son Richard succeeded—and married heiress Matilda Legh. Richard died in 1380. Their son, like his grandfather, also distinguished himself in French battles. The eldest of *his* four sons 'Sir John' inherited in 1421, and Sir Alexander followed.

In 1368, Thomas-del-Booth, close relation of the Radcliffe's, built a stone bridge costing £30, on which was built a Chapel. This was probably the first stone bridge built in England. After the Reformation the Chapel was turned into a prison to hold the recusants during the time of Elizabeth and James. This bridge was demolished and another built in 1838. The old Salford bridge was re-named Victoria Bridge.

In 1475, came Sir William Radcliffe, who died within a month of both his sons in 1497. His grandson Alexander aged twenty-two inherited holding Ordsall fifty-one years, becoming High Sheriff four times.

Another Sir William followed, but he and his eldest son died of plague in 1568. John, a younger son succeeded, and died in 1590 leaving a large family who went to Court as they came of age. At this time Ordsall had a water-mill for corn, sawmill, and a brick kiln.

John's eldest son Alexander became engaged to Marie Radcliffe a cousin who was also at Court. Sir Alexander's eldest sister Margaret was a favourite maid-of-honour to Queen Elizabeth I wearing a dress priced at £180, which is equal to £5,000 these days.

Four of the brothers died between 1598-1599, of wounds and fever in Flanders. Margaret died shortly after of grief for her twin Alexander.

The Gunpowder Plot was said to have been planned at Ordsall Hall in 1605, but there is some doubt as to whether Guy Fawkes ever saw the building. They say 'truth is stranger than fiction'—but who knows the truth?

RUFFORD OLD HALL.

Sir John, the one surviving brother, remained at Ordsall for a time, and was Lancashire's representative in Parliament several times. He was unhappy in his home life and left, but was killed in France in 1627. His son Sir Alexander, the last Radcliffe to reside at Ordsall Hall, was brought up at Court by a distant cousin Robert Radcliffe, K.G. fifth Earl of Sussex, who arranged Alexander's marriage when the boy was only fifteen, to his daughter Jane. Two years later Alexander helped carry the robes of Charles I at the Coronation, a service for which he was made 'Knight of the Bath'.

The Radcliffes were Royalists, and Lord Strange and Lord Molyneux both stayed at Ordsall before the 'Civil War' battle at Salford Bridge in 1642. Sir Alexander was wounded at Edge Hill, and later imprisoned in the Tower. He returned to Ordsall in 1654 to die.

In the early 1640s part of the estate was mortgaged to Humphrey Chetham (See Chetham's Hospital and Library).

Expense becoming too great for the Radcliffes, in 1662 the whole estate was sold to wealthy puritan Colonel John Birch, and as he wished, his thirteen-year-old daughter Sarah married her cousin John Birch, thus inheriting.

Ordsall changed hands several times, then in 1704 was sold by an Alice Oldfield for £4,300 to John Stocke, and later sold again to Samuel Hill of Staffordshire for £13,000.

During 1871, F. J. Shields, the artist, and friend of the Pre-Raphaelites, lived in one section which he converted into a studio. Salford artist Edward Finley resides there now, working on the premises. Ordsall Hall became the property of Lord Egerton, of Tatton in 1883. In turn it became an antique, curiosity shop, working-men's club, then in 1896 Earl Egerton converted it into a Clergy Training School. In 1920, Maurice, fourth Lord Egerton of Tatton inherited.

St Cyprian's Church was built on the site of the old Chapel. This is now derelict and will probably soon be demolished.

The ghost of Sir John may still haunt Ordsall Hall, also Guy Fawkes, Catesby, and many others. People in the neighbourhood are reported to have seen lights passing from room to room. This phenomena has never been explained, perhaps the 'Lady in White' who is said to haunt the premises, is searching for something—or some*one*, and who is she? The Lady who was said to have been bricked up in the wall? But they say the walls couldn't hold her, unless she was already invisible, otherwise she wouldn't stand the ghost of a chance.

Ordsall was damaged during the second world war, part of it which was used as a wireless station was damaged by fire, but the 'Old Soldier' still survives.

In 1959, Salford Corporation bought the Hall, and in 1963 started adapting it to a Museum. During excavations in the moat area fragments of high quality pottery of the sixteenth and seventeenth centuries have been found, also fragments of the most expensive Venetian glass, presumably from goblets.

The Historic Buildings Council, which is doing so much to save these interesting places, has contributed £9,000 towards restoration costs and promised about £12,000.

Some people may say Ordsall Hall has seen better days, let's hope it will even see *better*.

OSBALDESTON HALL

THIS ancient Hall dates from Anglo-Saxon times, and in 1063 was the private residence of an Anglo-Saxon Thane. It became the home of King Oswald, of Northumbria, Oswald being another form of the name Osbaldeston (Oswalds Tun) tun meaning the homestead on his estate north-west of Blackburn. This Hall stands on land which was once part of the 'geld island' of the King as in this ancient verse:

> Much pleasure hadst thou Oswald
> When dwelling in this region,
> Thou wert King of the Northumbrians
> Now of all the land holdest thou dominion
> Thou art commander in the place called Marcelde.

Marcelde is a corruption of Maggelde which means Majesty's geld island. Osbaldeston belongs to Maggelde.

The manor estate of Osbaldeston was portion of the great fee of Clitheroe, and in 1311 was named as appendant to the dower of the Countess of Lincoln, the widow of Earl Henry de Lascy.

In the days when the County was uncultivated and wild the earliest of the Osbaldestons to be recorded was Hugh, who lived in the time of Richard I. He was succeeded by Ailsi (or Eilfi) his son, who also had a son Hugh who was lord of the manor in 1245. A younger son Adam de Sunderland's children took the name de Wynkedelai (Winkley). Eilfi's children brought four different surnames into being: Osbaldeston, Winkley, Sunderland and Balderstone, Balderstone and Sunderland being within the manor. The son Winkley gave all his land in Sunderlandsholme with the woods pertaining to the manor to the monks of Sawley, for the salvation of his soul and that of his wife. Another son of Eilfi called Benedict, was Vicar of Preston in 1243. In direct line from Eilfi through another son came Simon de Balderstone who was also known as Simon de Burlegh (Birley) who in 1310 was High Sheriff and had lands in Yorkshire and Westmorland.

After a hundred years we have Sir John Osbaldeston who was knighted in 1415 by Henry V before the battle of Agincourt.

Much later came Sir Alexander Osbaldeston as lord of the manor. He was aged twenty-six in 1507, excelled himself in battle, and was knighted at Flodden. After rebuilding Sunderland Hall he gave it to his second son Richard, and built Oxendale Hall for another son.

Sir Alexander Osbaldeston, Knight, was Sheriff of Lancashire in 1527, John, his eldest son succeeded. He was a Captain in the Earl of Shrewsbury's army, and fought in Scotland. He married Jane, daughter of Thomas Stanley, the first Earl of Derby. They had a son Edward, who had a son John. This was the John Osbaldeston who in 1593 built the large stone barn. The date 1593 with his initials and those of relatives being carved on a stone over the main door at rear of Hall.

John's son Edward inherited in the reign of Elizabeth I. He was knighted by James I at Hoghton Tower, probably on the same occasion as the 'Sir Loin'.

During the Tudor and early Stuart reigns the Osbaldestons were one of the most distinguished families in Lancashire, several were knighted, and they formed a Chantry in Blackburn Parish Church.

This Domesday Manor House originally consisted

OLD HALL, RUFFORD.   Old Print.

RUFFORD HALL.   Old Print.

of two wings and a central portion. It was once surrounded by an earth fence, some of which can still be seen, and was also protected by a moat on three sides with the river on the fourth. It was said to have been a magnificent place during the reign of the first Stuart. Over the Large Drawing Room fireplace the family arms were carved and the initials of John, Edward, Margaret, and Maud Osbaldeston.

In the Court Room unmoveable red blood stains told their tale of tragedy. It was said that while a large family gathering was in process various arguments arose which developed into anger. The feast ended and drinks were plentiful, and tongues loosened. Sir Edward's brother Thomas challenged his brother-in-law to a duel. The family managed to intervene, but they met again later in the Court Room. Thomas Osbaldeston drew his sword and slew his brother-in-law Edward Walsh. For this he forfeited his lands. Tradition said the room was haunted by the ghost of Edward Walsh who visited the scene of conflict during the night, with raised hands, and blood streaming from his chest, but this ghost seems to have finally vanished into thin air, as the present owner's sister lived there thirteen years without making his acquaintance. However the blood stains remained until 1946, when new floor boards had to be put in. Quite recently a Lady Robinson who had been a Miss Walsh and was a descendant of Edward Walsh and his wife of Osbaldeston, visited the Hall in the hope of seeing the bloodstains of her ancestor, but was too late.

Sir Edward was married to Mary Farington of Hutton Grange. He was educated in France, and highly skilled in mathematics. He also excelled in fencing, riding and had many other accomplishments. Returning from travels in Italy he brought a plasterer to build the ornate fireplace in the Court Room (the first of its kind in the country) on this are the initials M.O. and E.O. He also brought and set the seed of the great Spanish chestnut tree, which is described as being of enormous girth. Sir Edward gave £500 for St Paul's Cathedral, which was a large sum in those days.

The estate eventually passed to Alexander Osbaldeston who died in 1747, without issue.

This Hall is not however without ghosts but they are of the gentle and retiring kind. One known as The Red Monk is thought to have been around since Anglo-Saxon times when Ailsi, son of Hugh was in residence and monks used to farm the land—he must know every inch of the Hall by this time. I wonder what or whom he is seeking?

Osbaldeston Hall is also haunted by the ghost of a Blue Lady. How charming to have a ghost in an 'Alice Blue Gown'. This lady's presence is unexplained and she must remain a mystery.

The stone fireplace was removed from the Banqueting Hall soon after the first world war, and rebuilt in the Entrance Hall, together with the oak panelling.

Osbaldeston Hall still remains a private residence. In 1942 the estate was purchased by Mr I. H. Lavery, who made many improvements. Worm eaten and rotten panelling was removed and replaced, a new oaken staircase was put in, and a beautiful carving of a Swiss Boy was flown specially from Switzerland in 1946 to decorate it.

On the death of Mr I. H. Lavery in 1949, the estate passed to his eldest son Mr Eric F. Lavery who is the present owner of Osbaldeston Hall.

PENNINGTON HALL

ANOTHER Lancashire Hall which has done a lot towards culture in its time is Pennington Hall, Leigh. The fast-changing landscape has lost many of its once important landmarks: Little Bolton Hall, Royle Hall, Danes House, and others have unfortunately disappeared, also Westleigh Old Hall where Ellen Ranicars who in her old age sat to have her portrait painted by Lancashire born artist George Romney. She died in 1799.

The first owners of Pennington Manor took their name from the township. Adam Pennington being Lord at the time (about 1294). He had a falconry in 1306. His two sons were Adam and Richard.

In 1625, the Hall was owned by Roger Bradshaw. His grandson succeeded in 1628, when aged seventeen. The Bradshaw estates were managed by Ralph Egerton who let the Hall to a widow Hannah Bate for a year, but she was ejected.

In 1723, an indentured mortgage for £1,200 was sealed, it charged Pennington Hall forty-seven acres, the mill, the tythe barn and a moiety of the tithes of the township with this payment.

Samuel Hilton, eldest son of James Hilton, sold Pennington Hall in 1807. He married Martha Clowes, daughter of banker-merchant Samuel Clowes of Broughton. He became High Sheriff of the County in 1811. In 1840 James Pownall a silk manufacturer lived in this Hall, and later became a magistrate.

In 1920 Pennington Hall was donated to the Corporation of Leigh by George Shaw Ltd., Bedford Brewery, and the grounds opened to the public. They were considerably extended. Part of the Hall was opened in 1928 as a Museum and Art Gallery, and an exhibition held consisting of a collection of Chinese Pottery and Porcelain loaned by a Mr John Hilditch of Manchester. A collection of specimens of Natural History and pictures and sculpture loaned by Salford City Council, and also a collection of old machinery used many years ago in handloom weaving silk, the gift of the late Mr George Hilton.

Pennington Hall did a great deal to encourage and help artists, and it was a great loss to the people of Leigh and elsewhere when it was demolished, but like others will still be remembered.

PLATT HALL

PLATT HALL, Rusholme, known as the 'Gallery of English Costume', is a Georgian House built in 1764, by the Worsley family, whose home it remained for many years.

This building of red brick stands out against the complementary green of the adjoining Platt Fields park-land, which was acquired by the Manchester Corporation after having been originally looked after by the Parks Committee. Platt Hall was taken over by the Art Galleries Committee Manchester, and opened as a branch gallery in 1927.

Examples of Georgian interior design can be seen in the Entrance Hall, and Staircase, also the Reception Room.

Until 1940, having been the headquarters of the Rutherston Loan Scheme, which served educational institutions throughout the north of England, it was used for war purposes, but in 1947, was re-opened to the public, as a Gallery of English Costume. Thus

SMITHILLS HALL.
Permission of Bolton Museum.

SMITHILLS HALL.
Courtyard from South.

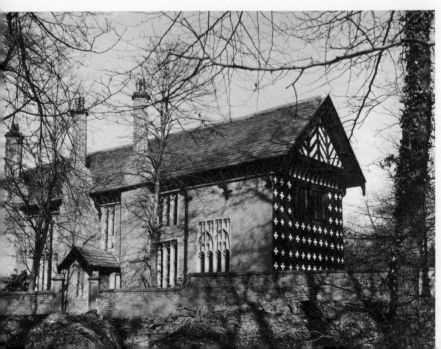

SAMLESBURY HALL.
Photograph, Reginald Dart.

Platt Hall became the first building in the country to be devoted solely to that particular branch of Art. This decision was made possible through the offer to Manchester, of the vast collection illustrating English-women's dress from the eighteenth century to about 1956, formed by Dr C. Willett Cunnington. An appeal for public subscriptions was successful, and together with a contribution from the Gallery's purchasing fund, the committee was enabled to acquire the collection, which has been added to by purchases and gifts. An interesting one being a group of eighteenth century costumes from the wardrobe of Thomas Carill-Worsley, who was the adopted son of the Worsley family who built the Hall. These costumes were presented by Mrs Tindal Carill-Worsley, his great-great-granddaughter.

How fashions have changed over the years can be seen here in Platt Hall, but how the Ladies of 1764, would have blushed and shivered at the very idea of wearing a mini skirt doesn't bear thinking about.

RADCLIFFE TOWER

R ADCLIFFE TOWER, was at one time considered to be one of the most important manorial residences in the county of Lancaster. The town and parish of Radcliffe is in the southern division of Lancaster and in the Bury union, seven miles N.N.W. of Manchester and 2½ miles S.S.W. of Bury. It is not definitely known at what date an original building was erected but Richard Radcliffe, High Sheriff of the County in 32 Edward III (1358), was of Radcliffe Tower, as was his predecessor William de Radcliffe one of the Knights of the Grand Inquest, 13 John (1211-12).

In 4 Henry IV (1403), this House was rebuilt and embattled. The imposing tower was of stone strongly grouted, with a communicating door to the house. Beneath the castellated rampart on the top tower at a depth of roughly four feet was a covering of lead. And over the Great Entrance door of the tower from each of the three storeys, a funnel, resembling an ancient chimney was there for a *very* unpleasant purpose. The domestic garrison used to keep the enemy at bay by pouring boiling pitch upon him. Too warm a welcome!

The last owner was the Earl of Wilton who sold the materials and let the land to Messrs R. Bealey & Sons, bleachers, when the building was demolished to make room for a row of cottages for the workers. And so the mighty became humble. The venerable pile of ruins were a constant reminder of the strongly built habitations of our forefathers for many long years, but time leaves its mark, and then obliterates it. Radcliffe Tower is now a memory of the past.

RUFFORD OLD HALL

R UFFORD OLD HALL stands six miles North of Ormskirk, amidst a rural setting of many varieties of beautiful old trees, and is bounded on the East by the Leeds and Liverpool Canal.

This superb example of a mediaeval half-timbered House is believed to have been built by Robert Hesketh who held the manor from 1463-1490. Previously the holder's were the Fittons of Great Harwood then it passed by marriage to the Heskeths. Sir William Heskayte Knt., Lord of Heskayte and Beconsawe in 1276, was fourth in descent from Richard Hesketh of

Hesketh. He married Dame Maude, daughter and co-heiress of Richard Fitton of Great Harwood, Martholme, and Rufford, nephew of Sir Richard Fitton of Pownall in Cheshire. Their grandson Sir John de Heskayte Knt., Lord of Heskayte and Rufford, married Alice, daughter and sole-heiress of Edmund Fytton, Lord of *half* the manor of Rufford, thus the whole of Rufford and the other Fytton estates passed by inheritance to their eldest son Sir William de Heskayte, Lord of Rufford, Heskaithe, Beconsawe, Great Harwood, and Tottleworth, who fought at Crecy in 1346, and was Knight of the Shire in 1360.

In the year 1463, Robert Hesketh of Rufford inherited. This Robert Hesketh is the one previously referred to as the possible builder of Rufford Hall. He died in 1490, and his eldest son Thomas Hesketh Esq., succeeded him. Thomas's first wife was Elizabeth Fleming of Croston, from whom he obtained a divorce which was confirmed in 1497 by Pope Alexander VI. Elizabeth later married Thurstan Hall, and later, in 1501 Thomas Hesketh married Grace, daughter of Richard Towneley. Their only son William died before his father, childless. Therefore Thomas made his natural son Robert the heir, and also provided funds for many causes: The Rufford* Chantry; almshouses, school etc. Thomas died in 1523.

Sir Robert Hesketh Knt., fought in Henry VIII's campaigns including the 'Battle of the Spurs' in 1539, and served the King in France for which he was Knighted. He married Grace, daughter of Sir John Towneley of Towneley, and died in 1539. Sir Thomas Heskaith Knt., their eldest son inherited, and was knighted at the Coronation of Queen Mary in 1553. Fought in Scotland at the Seige of Leith; was High Sheriff of Lancashire in 1563; and was imprisoned in 1581 under suspicion of practising Roman Catholicism after the accession of Queen Elizabeth I. Sir Thomas was married to Alice, daughter of Sir John Holcrofte of Holcrofte. They had three sons and two daughters. Sir Thomas also had two illegitimate sons.

Richard, the third son was involved in the Lancashire Plot to bring Ferdinando the fifth Earl of Derby onto the English throne. This Richard was executed at St Albans. As stated in the chapter on Knowsley Hall, Ferdinando was said to have been poisoned in 1594. Richard's elder brother Thomas Hesketh, born at Martholme in 1561, practised medicine at Clitheroe, and was a botanist.

Robert Heskaith, the eldest brother, succeeded to the family estates in 1587. He had been contracted into marriage in 1567, to Mary, daughter of Sir George Stanley of Cross Hall; sat in Parliament as a member for Lancashire in 1597, and was High Sheriff of the County 1599-1600. They had five sons and three daughters. The eldest daughter Holcroft married Roger Dodsworth, the antiquary. Robert Heskaith died in 1620.

Thomas Heskaith Esq. the eldest son succeeded on the death of his father, and was High Sheriff of Lancashire 1629-30. In 1631 declining a knighthood he was fined fifty pounds. He married three times yet had no children. His brother Robert Heskaith Esq., succeeded.

In 1652, when Robert was about eighty years of age, he was threatened with the withdrawal of his estate by the Parliamentary authorities. His wife was Margaret, daughter of Alexander de Standish. They had one son Robert Heskaith Esq., who died before his father in 1651, and whose wife Lucy, was daughter of Alexander Rigby of Middleton. They had a son

SPEKE HALL.

Painting, Margaret Chapman.

Thomas Hesketh who was born in 1647. On the instruction of his trustees, or with their consent, the North East brick wing of Rufford Hall was built. This bears Thomas's initials with the date 1662.

Thomas, a Protestant, married Sydney, daughter of Sir Richard Grosvenor, of Eaton. Their great-grandson Sir Thomas Hesketh, Bart., was created the first baronet in 1761. His marriage to Harriet Cowper, daughter of Ashley Cowper, brought the poet William Cowper into the family (who was Harriet's first cousin). Sir Thomas Hesketh built the New Hall which was later enlarged by the third baronet and used as the family seat.

Sir Thomas George Hesketh the fifth baronet, in 1846 married the Lady Anna Maria Arabella Fermor, sister and heiress of George, the fifth and last Earl of Pomfret. Thus the Heskeths of Rufford inherited the Fermor estate of Easton Neston, Northamptonshire, and the name Fermor was added to Hesketh.

Sir Thomas Fermor-Hesketh the eighth baronet was created a baron in 1935. He lived at the Old Hall spending much time on its preservation, and in 1936 presented the home that he loved Rufford Old Hall, with endowments and about eleven acres of garden and land to the National Trust.

The Old Hall is now a Village Museum, and houses relics of ancient local life of the people, *for* the people. In this way they can look back into the past way of living and compare it with the present.

The building at one time formed an East and West wing joined together by a central Hall. The West wing was destroyed centuries ago, and the East wing was reconstructed in brick in 1662 as stated before. This was partially rebuilt in 1821.

The Great Hall is almost in its original state, and possibly the best preserved example of its kind and day. This measures 46 feet 6 inches long, 22 feet 6 inches wide, and 18 feet high to the wallplate.

A remarkable massive moveable screen of carved oak of the fifteenth century commands attention. At the West End of the Manor the Lord of the Manor used to dine on a high table while the retainers had their meal in the main part of the hall. There is a long bench against the wall with doors at either side which used to lead into the private wing. The wall between may have been covered with tapestry, and above, a curved canopy conceals a secret chamber.

At the North-West corner of the hall is a beautiful bay window which in stained glass bears the Stanley arms.

The hammer-beam roof in this Great Hall is outstanding and typical of its time. Here are figures of Angels most of which have lost their wings. Angels without wings they may be but they have not lost their beauty.

The Drawing Room measures 44 feet long by 17 feet wide, and although this seems a fairly modern room it has a sixteenth century roof with a spy-hole.

The fine oak furniture at Rufford Old Hall was made for the Hesketh family about seventeenth and eighteenth centuries. There are court-cupboards one of which bears the crest of the Heskeths and is dated 1661, chests, refectory tables; old oak settles. A small oak table bears the initials of Thomas Hesketh and date 1673 with legend 'Amor Vincit Omnia'. There is also an interesting collection of arms and armour.

In the Village Museum founded in 1939 by Mr Philip Ashcroft of Rufford, and which he presented to the National Trust in 1946, are many fascinating things. A dug-out canoe (c. 100 B.C.) which was found in the Martin Mere; agricultural implements and tools; a great cheese-press; Staffordshire Pottery figures; a glass witch bowl to keep the 'Lancashire Witches' away, and costumes and toys of Victorian days. This Museum is housed in four rooms of the 1821 wing and the gallery of the Carolean wing.

In nearby Rufford Parish Church, (which was built in 1869 on the site of an older Chapel), are memorials to various members of the Hesketh family. A tablet to the memory of Sir Thomas Hesketh (died 1778) bears a verse by poet William Cowper.

The New Hall is now a hospital, but the Rufford Old Hall with its mullioned windows, although altered in some ways, still remains as a most interesting place of ancient times.

The Hesketh family arms bears a double-headed eagle.

SAMLESBURY HALL

THIS mediaeval half-timbered Manor House, the earliest part of which dates back to 1325, is situated between Blackburn and Preston.

During the early part of the reign of Henry II, Gospatric de Samlesbury's ancestral home was surrounded by green fields and a forest of oak trees. From these trees were taken the gigantic powerful timbers used to form the framework of the structure of the Great Hall. Here at the time when rushes were spread on the floor where servants and retainers used to sleep—between watching the flames leaping from an open fire in the centre, from which smoke slowly found a way out through a hole in the roof (about mid-thirteenth century) lived Gospatric de Samlesbury. He had three great-granddaughters, Cicely, Margery, and Elizabeth who married Robert de Holland, who together with John De Ewyas, who married Cicely, became Lords of Samlesbury in right of their wives.

When John De Ewyas died he was succeeded by his son Nicholas, and when *he* died about 1320, his share of the manor passed to his daughter Alicia, Cicely's granddaughter. She was married to Sir Gilbert Southworth, (and the Hall remained in the family's possession for about 350 years). He died in 1346, and was succeeded by his eldest surviving son Thomas, Knight of the Shire for Lancaster 1380. His son Sir John Southworth succeeded, he married Margaret de Hoghton.

In 1398, the Duke of Lancaster retained him as an Esquire for life, at a fee of £10. He travelled with the Duke to France contracting to supply fifty archers for the French campaign, in return for £113.15.0d. per annum. John Southworth died in 1415 during the seige of Harfleur.

Thomas de Southworth inherited. He married Joan, widow of Sir Thomas Sherbourne, sister of the Bishop of Lichfield, and half-sister to the Archbishop of York. This Thomas built the domestic Chapel in 1420. He died in 1432. (One of the Southworths fought in the battle of Agincourt as an archer.)

In 1546, Sir Thomas Southworth reconstructed the house, building hearths with chimneys and panelling walls which were originally of wattle and daub.

Sir John (1546-1595) followed. He was very distinguished and in high military command during the early years of the reign of Elizabeth I. Sir John Southworth was Sheriff of Lancashire in 1562, and the owner of several estates, and lands in eighteen other

SPEKE HALL.
Old Print.

STONEYHURST.
by J. M. W. Turner.

towns. He was arrested in 1581 for harbouring. His son paid a fine of £500, and entered into sureties for his good conduct.

In a small room 10 feet square, known as the 'Oratory' were found stains on the floor said to be the blood of a murdered Priest. This remained for two-hundred years, when Frederick Baynes, High Sheriff of Lancashire had it re-floored in the 1890s. Above this room is a 'hide' or 'bolt hole'. The Southworths remained loyal to the faith of their forefathers, and the Hall was the haunt of many seminary Priests. The Jesuit preacher 'Campion' stayed here in the Easter of 1581, a few months later he was captured and executed.

Sir John's eldest son Thomas (1595-1617) succeeded and *his* grandson Thomas followed. He lived until 1624, leaving two sons who died in their teens, and two daughters. Their uncle, John Southworth, after twenty years of lawsuits etc, inherited next. This had taken much of the family fortune, and in 1666 John Southworth sold Samlesbury Park for £318. He had fourteen children, and died in 1676. His third son Edward succeeding. Who through enforced circumstances sold Samlesbury Hall in 1678, to Thomas Braddyll for £3,150, who later let the Hall to hand-loom-weavers as tenements.

Thomas Richard Gale Braddyll (1776-1862) went bankrupt, and in 1850 the Hall which had been converted into an Ale-House, was sold to John Cooper of Penwortham, Nr Preston, under its new name of 'The Braddyll Arms'. John Cooper rented it to a Mrs Harrison of Bradford who started a girls school.

In 1862, on coming into the hands of Mr Joseph Harrison Esq., of Blackburn, Samlesbury Hall was restored inside and out. He replaced the old staircase with the present one which bears his crest and date 1865, on the newel posts. Samlesbury became the home of his son William who through financial difficulties ended his life.

It next became the residence of Fred Baynes J.P. Mayor of Blackburn (1896-7) and High Sheriff of the County 1900. He left in 1909, and in 1924 a firm of builders bought the site with a view to demolition.

A meeting was held at the instigation of the 'Ancient Monuments Society' and an appeal brought £5,000, the full purchase price was guaranteed by a body of trustees, and the Hall was purchased in 1925.

A Society was formed in 1928, called the 'Friends of Samlesbury' the President being Bishop P. M. Herbert, with trustees T. B. Lewis, J. W. Marsden, F. Morton, H. Whittaker and Dr Davies, and they saved and helped preserve a great Historic House.

In 1927, workmen employed in restoration discovered in the region of the old moat, the jaw-bone of a wild boar. The boar's head was very popular on the table in the old days, and on King James Is visit to Hoghton Tower in 1617 a wild boar pie was on the menu.

In the Large Dining Room at Samlesbury a richly carved cornice bears the Tudor Rose. Above the doors are two carved wooden portraits of King Henry VIII and one of his Queens. On one side of the fireplace is a window displaying the arms of the Southworths, and in the other, those of the Braddylls. The Tudor fireplace is decorated with two shields, one bearing the arms of Sir Richard Hoghton of Hoghton Tower, High Sheriff of Lancashire 1540; the other those of Sir Thomas Langton of Walton-le-Dale, Knighted in 1533, Sheriff of Lancashire 1556 and 1567. On the upper centre of fireplace is the flowing Bull's Head

crest of the Southworth's. Along breadth of mantel is carved Thomas Southworth Kt, and a date Ao Dni MCCCCC XLV 1545.

The Hall is now L-Shaped in plan, but was no doubt once quadrangular enclosing a courtyard.

Tradition says that during Sir John's later years, one of his daughters became attached to the heir of a neighbouring knight's house, her father would not give his consent to the marriage, saying: 'No daughter of his should ever marry the son of a family which had deserted its ancestral faith.' He forbade them to meet, but they managed many secret interviews and decided to elope. Unfortunately the girl's brother overheard the plans and hiding in some bushes rushed out and slew the girl's lover. The body was secretly buried in the grounds of the domestic Chapel. Lady Dorothy was sent to a Convent abroad, where she went out of her mind, constantly repeating the name of her murdered lover. Thus she died. A skeleton was discovered near the Hall walls years afterwards.

Legend also has it that on clear calm evenings a 'Lady in White' may be seen gliding along the gallery and corridors and out into the grounds, where she is met by a handsome young knight who after kneeling to welcome Dorothy, accompanies her in the walks. On reaching a certain place which is thought to have been the lover's grave, the ghosts stand still, wail softly in despair, then embracing, slowly rise into the blue sky and vanish. A White Lady is said to still haunt the M6 motorway not far away.

Samlesbury Hall has its ghosts, and very beautiful ones too. Let's hope they find greater happiness in the Spirit world than they had on earth. The White Lady was reported to have been seen in 1878, by a Colonel. Gospatric de Samlesbury may still haunt his ancestral home also; this remains to be seen.

SMITHILLS HALL

THIS ancient building is situated two miles north-west of Bolton, in a beautiful park, on the slopes of Smithills Moor, at the edge of a steep cliff, and like other defensive Halls was originally protected by a moat.

The first owners of Smithills Hall seem to have been the Knights Hospitallers, from whom it was held by Richard de Hulton, who married twice, and made the Manor over to his second wife's great-nephew William de Radcliffe, son of Robert, who was the younger son of Richard of Radcliffe Tower in the time of Edward III. It then passed to Raphe Radcliffe, (D. 1406), Knight of the Shire in two Parliaments 1398 and 1404, then to the second Sir Raphe, Knight of the Shire in 1413, 1422, and 1426. And next to his son, the third Sir Raphe, whose nephew another Ralph or Raphe, the son of his half-brother Edmund succeeded him.

Next, in 1485, Smithills Hall passed to Cecily, daughter of the last Ralph de Radcliffe, who married her second cousin John Barton, grandson of the third Sir Raphe. In 1516, *their* son Andrew Barton inherited, he extended the building considerably. The Hall was next owned by Andrew's son Robert, then by his widow Margery, who later married Sir Richard Shuttleworth, Chief Justice of Chester, whose youngest brother Thomas lived with them, acting as Steward of the Estates.

Thomas married Anne, daughter of Richard Lever, of Little Lever, in 1586. They had three sons and three daughters:

TRAFFORD HALL.   Old Print.

TONGE HALL, PRESTWICH.

Richard, the eldest son, born in 1587, succeeded to his uncle's estates. He was knighted, and became a leading parliamentary magistrate during the Commonwealth.

Lady Margery Shuttleworth died in 1592. Her brother-in-law Thomas, died in 1593, and Sir Richard Shuttleworth in 1599.

Ralph, the son of Margery by Robert Barton, inherited Smithills Hall, built the west wing and the three gabled wing adjoining it. Thomas Barton was the next owner.

In 1723, the estate was sold to Joseph Byrom, of Manchester. He added to the west wing, and probably had the gardens landscaped.

In 1801, Peter Ainsworth bought Smithills for the sum of £21,000. He lived till 1807, and Richard Ainsworth, a later owner died 1833.

The last owner was Captain Nigel Ainsworth, who held the Hall until 1938, when it was sold to the County Borough of Bolton, who after the 1939-45 War, with the help of Government aid, have restored the Hall to something of its original beauty.

The Great Hall, which is the oldest part of the building, measures about 35 feet by 25 feet, and its open-timbered roof with 'quatrefoil' decoration, is most impressive. Many years ago the Great Hall would have a dais at the east end where the Lord of the Manor sat with his family. This has recently been restored and furnished mostly with furniture of the Stuart Period. And with adjoining rooms was built about 1350.

The fine linenfold panelling in the fascinating With-Drawing Room dates from early Tudor times. Other panels show carved heads and devices from the Barton's 'Coat of Arms' and in a certain panel is Andrew's 'Rebus' showing the initials A and B with a 'tun' or barrel of ale crossed by a bar of wood. In Tudor times they often used to draw the name thus, as a pun, instead of writing it.

The Barton's badge was an 'acorn' and oak leaf, no doubt because of the vast forest from which the oak beams were taken for the building. Thus the mighty oak has given strength and beauty to Smithills Hall.

During the reign of Queen Mary, about 1554, a young Curate named George Marsh was brought before Robert Barton the magistrate, for examination as a heretic. Tradition says that to emphasize a remark in declaring his Protestant faith, he stamped his foot while being led from the justice room. The foot sank into the stone pavement, leaving an imprint ever to remain. (A case of leaving an impression by putting his foot in it.) The prisoner was taken to Lathom Hall, where a Bishop condemned him to death. He was burnt on 24th April 1555, at Spittal Broughton, just outside Chester. The mark of the footprint can be seen at the entrance to the Chapel passage. Hot-Foot? Well! the colour is dark *red*. The story goes that once, two or three young men who were living in the House, moved the stone for a joke and threw it into the woods. That night the inhabitants were disturbed by strange and terrifying noises. The stone was quickly restored with much reverence, and the noises ceased.

The Chapel was destroyed by fire on 10th November 1856, and rebuilt in 1858. We may not all leave our footprint in the sands of time but we do help to form the pattern of life.

We cling to our ancient buildings mostly because of their historical associations, and are rightly proud of them. If there is a ghost which thrills us to the marrow, so much the better. Here we can recapture the past 'bad old days' when people were tortured, beheaded, hanged-drawn-and-quartered, burnt at the stake, and other gruesome things. And so we realize and appreciate how much Britain has progressed. 'Long may these Houses stand!' The future of Smithills Hall is assured, as it is now scheduled an 'Ancient Monument'.

SPEKE HALL

SPEKE HALL, stands seven miles from the busy City centre of Liverpool, on the edge of the Airport, overlooking the River Mersey.

Quadrangular in form, this old family Mansion in its beautiful woodland setting is a very fine example of the black-and-white half-timbered method of construction, and has a roof covered with the old grey stone slates used in the Gothic Period. But although dating back to the fifteenth century, an earlier House of sandstone previously stood on or near the site of the present building, the History of the Manor going back to the Domesday Survey of 1086, where it is described as 'The Manor of Spec', one of several properties held by Uctred since 1066, or before. Previously in 1170 it is further recorded that it had been the property of the Master Foresters of Lancashire.

Shortly after the Conquest Speke Hall was held by Roger Gerneth, who gave two carucates in Spec to Richard de Mulas or Molyneux. (A 'carucate' meaning as much land as a team can plough in a year.)

Annota, sole daughter and heiress of Benedict Gernot, conveyed the Manor to her husband Adam Molyneux in the reign of Edward I. It was next owned by his son Roger, and daughter, who married William de Haselwal. Speke passed to Jane, daughter of Sir William Molyneux, who was a descendant of Roger. Jane married Robert de Erneys, of Chester.

Two of the sons of Alan le Noreis, of Formby, Liverpool, married the two daughters of Sir Patric de Haselwal—Margery and Nicola. The girls' father divided his half holding between the two, but it was later owned by Nicola and her husband John, whose descendant Sir Henry le Noreis succeeded to the estates in 1372. He later married Alice, the only daughter of Roger Erneys, thus bringing her half-holding into the estate.

The 'overlordship', which had been retained by the Molyneux's passed to the Bolds of Bold, the Charnocks, then the Norreys. In 1490, Speke Hall became the property of Sir William Norreys, who originated the building of the present Hall, demolishing the sandstone House. His son Henry followed as Lord of the Manor. In 1524 *his* eldest son William succeeded and made great alterations to the building which up to then had even an open fire. He also extended considerably, adding the Great Parlour. William was very creative, obviously—he had nineteen children. His son Edward succeeded him in 1568, and he also made additions to the building. An archway leading into the garden bears the initials of Edward and his wife with the date 1605. Their son William succeeded in 1606, and was later knighted. He unfortunately ran into debt, sold the Chester estates, and mortgaged his Speke holdings to John Fleming, of Rydal (his son-in-law). Sir William died in 1626, and his son (also named William), a staunch Royalist, succeeded him. He fought for Charles against the Parliamentary forces.

TURTON TOWER.

Painting, Margaret Chapman.

In 1650, the Commonwealth Parliament seized all the Speke estates. A year later William renounced the Roman Catholic faith. In 1662 his son Thomas regained the estates.

In 1699, a later Lord of the Manor Sir William, was appointed Ambassador Extraordinary to the Great Mogul.

The last of the male heirs was Richard Norres who died in 1731, and the estates were conveyed by his niece Mary Norres, to Lord Sidney Beauclerc. His grandson Charles, in 1797 sold the Manor to Richard Watt a West India Merchant, of Liverpool. Speke Hall was then in an extremely dilapidated condition, and Richard Watt spent a large sum on restorations. Having made a fortune in Jamaica he had on returning to Liverpool, established the firm 'Watt & Walker' in Hanover Street. His nephew Richard Watt Esq., of Bishop Burton, in Yorkshire, succeeded him in 1849. Speke Hall later passed to Adelaide Watt, the grandson's only daughter who died unmarried in 1921. She left the estate in trust for members of the Norris family for twenty-one years, after which it was held in trust for a Mr Hewson.

In August 1942, Speke Hall was given to the National Trust, who leased it to the Liverpool Corporation for ninety-nine years.

In the Courtyard of Speke Hall are two large Yew trees which are over four-hundred years old, named Adam and Eve. They no doubt live up to their names in the autumn.

Entering the Great Hall, with its flat ceiling, one's attention is arrested by a remarkable fireplace, with a massive oak mantelbeam 16 feet long and 2 feet thick. This was no doubt the work of Sir William Norreys who built the screens in the Great Hall. On the Ingle Nook are mouldings of the Perpendicular Period. There is some elaborate plaster work and carving, and also magnificent old carved furniture, rich panelling, and armour. A Jacobean Canopy said to have been presented to Sir Henry Norreys (the son of Sir William), by Henry VIII for military service at Flodden Field, is believed to have come from the King of Scotland's palace.

The Great Parlour has a striking Italian stucco ceiling which dates from the sixteenth century. Here is a most interesting overmantel with a carved record representing three generations of the Norreys family. This depicts the second Sir William (1524-68), his two wives, nineteen children, and other important members.

A door leads into the gardens through a porch which is the only addition made by the third Sir William Norreys. A shield on the outer door bears his initials and those of Eleanor Molyneux his wife, and the date 1613.

The Morning Room with its eighteenth century blue and white Dutch tiles is very fascinating, and has an overmantel depicting the old Royal Palace at the Hague. There is also a Regency chiming clock dated about 1800, and one by William Roskell dated 1830s.

The State Bedroom was probably the sleeping quarters of Charles I in 1630, although there is no actual proof of this.

The Green Bedroom, known as the Priest's Room, is entered by a secret passage through a small panel on the south of the fireplace, behind which is a vertical ladder leading eventually to the Priest's Hole.

The Tapestry Room is known as the 'Haunted Chamber'. It is said that a Lady of the Beauclerk family while living at Speke Hall, very upset at her husband's financial ruin, after throwing her child through the window into the moat, committed suicide in the Great Hall.

Every family has its trials and tragedies, but this one has lasted well beyond a lifetime, for the Lady's unhappy ghost is still said to haunt this room. A Flemish cradle bearing the date 1631 is worthy of note.

These Halls are a great and noble heritage, we must treat them with the respect which the ancient deserve—Halls or Humans. Thus we retain a dignity which is truly British, and irreplaceable.

STONYHURST HALL

STONYHURST, the famous Roman Catholic School, stands on the slopes of Long Ridge Fell.

Originally the home of the Shireburnes, Sir Richard, the Elizabethan, started the building, but on the death of his son abandoned it. His successor, Sir Nicholas, completed the task, and *his* daughter the Duchess of Norfolk resided there. After her death this turreted house with its four tall cupolas gradually deteriorated, and was offered to some Roman Catholic refugees from France. Many Priests and Scholars brought treasured relics making it also a Museum.

The four-storeyed entrance front bears the coat-of-arms of Sir Nicholas over the portals. Carved Stones from Whalley Abbey and a fourteenth century window have been added. In the Great Hall stands an oak table where Cromwell is said to have made his soldiers bed when staying overnight on his way to Preston.

The Gallery is made of sixteenth century timbers. There are alabaster tables, a cap embroidered in silver with the seal of Sir Thomas More, and on it the badge of St George, which he wore when Knight of the Garter and Lord Chancellor, and many other fascinating items.

In the Library are much treasured books, including the little Book of Hours which Mary Queen of Scots is said to have carried when she went to execution at Fotheringay. This has the words Maria Regina, and the arms of England and France on its cover. There is also a lock of her hair. So Stonyhurst is proud of owning an actual part of a Queen within its castle-like walls.

TONGE HALL

TONGE HALL was built about the time of Henry VIII and once stood in the Parish of Prestwich. Connected with the Langleys in a common descent from the Prestwich family of Prestwich (See Agecroft Hall). The Tonge Family of Tonge were descended from Thomas de Tonge, who was the son of Alice de Wolveley, an heiress of the Prestwich family.

The Tonges remained owners of Tonge Hall, where they lived until 1726, when the Estate was sold pursuant to the will of Jonathon Tonge, Gent., to Mr John Starky of Heywood for £4,350, and with other estates passed by the will of his grandson James Starky Esq., who died in 1846, to his relatives Mrs Hornby of St Michael's, and Joseph Langton Esq., of Liverpool.

Above: TURTON TOWER.
Old Print.

Below: TURTON TOWER.
Photograph, Reginald Dart.

TOWNELEY HALL

TOWNELEY HALL, Burnley, stands within its own beautiful park, ornamental gardens, tennis courts and golf course.

The name 'Towneley' probably originated from a 'tun' or town, and the lea—a field.

Beginning with the family history. After the Norman Conquest under the feudal system, estates were granted by the King to his barons in return for an oath of allegiance and an undertaking to provide a number of armed Knights, or their equivalent in money for each soldier in war time. The barons in turn sublet parts of their estates, and so it happened that Roger de Lacy, who held from King John the 'Honour of Clitheroe', granted in 1200, lands at Tunleia (Towneley), to Geoffrey, son of Robert, the Dean of Whalley, who was married to his daughter.

Geoffrey's grandson granted Towneley to his brother Richard, since when it became the permanent home of the Towneley family. Richard died in 1295. The next Richard de Towneley, Knight of the Shire, had a seat in the House of Commons, and was High Sheriff of Lancashire from 1375-79. His son John (1343-1399) also received the King's favour, but forfeited it. His son succeeded while quite a young boy. He fought at Agincourt in 1415. John, born the same year, next inherited. Isabella Shireburne of Stonyhurst became his wife, and they had six children, only one a girl. The sons founded the Hurstwood, Hapton, Barnside, Dutton, and Royle branches of the family. Nicholas, the third son, became a Reader and Bencher at Gray's Inn. Through him a branch of the family was founded in America. His eighth son married Elizabeth Cartaret, the widow of the Governor of New Jersey.

John's son Richard succeeded, and was knighted by Lord Stanley on the field of Hutton in 1482. His nine-year-old son followed. This John Towneley (1473-1541), built the Towneley domestic Chapel and Hapton Tower. The Chapel is of great architectural interest and beauty, and measures 33 feet by 18 feet. The Nave measures only about 12 feet high, with flat ceiling. The Chancel portion being nearly twice as high. On this roof are carvings of the grape-vine. Over the once Confessional Room door is a beautiful carved wooden shield bearing the crests of the Towneleys of Towneley, and Asshetons of Lever, dated 1601.

Sir John Towneley received his knighthood for services on the battlefield in Scotland, and in 1531 was Sheriff of Lancashire.

The next owner of Towneley Hall was Richard, who married Grace, the daughter and heiress of Sir Godfrey Foljambe, of Whalley, Derby and Bennett. Their son Richard, who was knighted at the 'Siege of Leith', married Francess, heiress of the Nocton estates, Lincolnshire, in 1536. He died (before his father) in 1554, and Mary, his only surviving daughter, inherited when aged thirteen. She married her cousin John Towneley of Gray's Inn. (This is the John (1528-1608) whose picture hangs in the Towneley Room, and who suffered so much for his religious beliefs.) His son Richard Towneley (1566-1629), who also suffered in a similar way, married Jane Assheton, the daughter of Ralph.

Charles (1600-1644), who was educated abroad, fought in Manchester during the 1642 Civil War for Charles I. He sought refuge from the Parliamentary forces at Towneley, later taking shelter in a gamekeeper's cottage near Dyneley, from where he rejoined the Royalist army at Wigan. Charles was killed in 1644, at Marston Moor, while fighting with Prince Rupert. Richard, his younger brother, through loyalty to the Stuart cause, was imprisoned and his goods confiscated. He later married the widow of Richard of Barnside and settled to live at Carr Hall, Nelson. Richard Towneley was known as the 'Transcriber', having translated and preserved many valuable historical documents. He was connected with the 'Lancashire Plot' in 1689-94, to restore James II to the throne. His grandson, (another Richard) took part in the 1715 Rising.

Francis, his brother, born 1709, was educated in France, and won distinction for military services under the French King. He returned to England joining the forces under Prince Charles Edward, and became Colonel of the Manchester Regiment. When the Prince's forces retreated to Scotland, Colonel Towneley tried without success to hold the City 'Carlisle' against the Royalist troops under the Duke of Cumberland. Colonel Francis was beheaded in 1746.

William Towneley, succeeded in 1735, but died in 1742 aged twenty-eight. His wife Cecilia, was daughter of Ralph Standish. Her eldest son Charles, inherited, and the Standish estates went to the second son. Charles, (1737-1805), was a great art lover and collector. A painting of him by Zoffany hangs in the gallery. The estate passed to his brother Edward Standish, then to his Uncle John. And next to his son Peregrine Edward Towneley (1772-1847), who was High Sheriff of Lancashire in 1828, and known for his great generosity. His eldest son Charles, (1803-1876) followed. He was a J.P., Deputy Lieutenant of the County, and High Sheriff, and like his father, a President of the Mechanic's Institute. Charles' brother John next inherited, but died within a very short time in (1878). His only son had died of fever in Italy the previous year. So the male line of this great family ended.

There were three daughters, co-heiresses of each brother Charles and John. Alice Mary, the youngest daughter of Colonel Charles Towneley inherited. Married to Lord O'Hagan, Lord Chancellor of Ireland in 1871, Lady O'Hagan was greatly respected for her kindness to the people. Finding Towneley Hall too expensive to maintain after the death of her husband, she went to live at the Hollins in 1902, and sold Towneley Hall to the Corporation of Burnley for a sum much less than its value. Her generosity has left a memorial of great beauty. Lady O'Hagan died in 1921.

Towneley Hall Art Gallery and Museum has a Great Hall which used to be a two storey building, but about 1725 this was converted into an Entrance Hall by Richard Towneley (1689-1735). Measuring 33 feet high, 42 feet long, and 28 feet wide, this is decorated in the neo-classical style by Vassali the Italian sculptor. Here is an 18 foot long banqueting table, and a settle, purchased from Barcroft Hall, Cliviger, by Charles Towneley. The very beautiful chandelier has over two thousand pieces of English hand-cut crystal. It was installed in 1960.

Towneley, which is still an Historic House, has a stone cantilever staircase complete with 'dog gate' which kept the dogs from exploring the upper rooms.

The Long Gallery, 85 feet in length, has a ceiling bearing initials of members of the family who lived in the fifteenth and sixteenth centuries. Here is the

WARDLEY HALL.

Painting, Margaret Chapman.

spiral staircase (now sealed) which once led through a 6 foot thick wall to the Chapel below. And no doubt used by Catholic Priests during unhappy times is the Priest's Hiding Place, where on climbing the staircase it is hard to believe it lies straight ahead.

The Art Gallery, contains paintings by Constable, Peter Lely, Fantin Latour, Gainsborough, J. M. Turner, and other masters. There is also an East Lancashire Regimental Room which holds many treasures.

Towneley Hall was originally built for defence, forming at one time a complete quadrangle of six-foot thick walls of stone and grout-work, four turrets at the angles supported by strong projecting butresses—truly castle-like.

The front door entering from quadrangle to the Great Hall, is very ancient, richly carved and ornamented. This bears the date A.D. M.D. XXX. The Porch is dated 1614.

On leaving Towneley Hall, it's almost like parting from an old friend who has stood the test of time and remained faithful to the family motto: 'Tenez le Vraye'—HOLD TO THE TRUTH.

THE TWO TRAFFORD HALLS

TRAFFORD OLD HALL stood on Chester Road, Old Trafford, between Trafford Bar and Henshaw's Institution for the Blind. The De Trafford family has been connected with the district since the Norman Conquest, and their home was on this site until the mid-seventeenth century when Sir Cecil Trafford bought Wiggleswick Hall and the estate.

He built Trafford Hall on the site of Wiggleswick Hall, and the estate became known as Trafford Park. The De Trafford family lived there until 1896 when Sir Humphrey de Trafford sold the estate to Trafford Park Estates Ltd., after the building of the Manchester Ship Canal.

Trafford Old Hall, of no architectural interest whatever, and in a rather dilapidated state, was demolished by the Corporation in 1939.

Trafford Hall in Trafford Park, now completely industrialized, stood empty for many years and was demolished by enemy action during the last war.

TURTON TOWER

TURTON TOWER, has a high situation on Chapeltown Road, Turton, in the neighbourhood of Bolton, and in the twelfth century belonged to Roger Fitz-Robert and to Henry, Duke of Lancaster. It was owned by the Lathom Family from the thirteenth century until 1420, when Elizabeth, daughter of John de Torbock married William Orrell.

In the year 1596, the tower was extensively altered by William, at the time when the workmen's pay was said to have been only one penny a day (The Good Old Days) one-armed bandits of today would be as rare as Venus de Milo on that amount.

The high imposing Tower measures about 46 feet long, and 28 feet wide, this was built square with the points of the compass, and originally had small mediaeval windows, but in 1596, William Orrell had them replaced by larger mullioned ones to give more light. The walls are of stone and about 4 feet thick. Older parts still retain the wood and plaster decorations characteristic of the early Tudor Period.

William's son and heir John, was extravagant and so the estate suffered. His brother (another William) succeeded him in 1626.

In 1628, the Tower was purchased at the sum of £4,000 from the last of the Orrells by Humphrey Chetham, founder of the Manchester Hospital and Library. In 1653, his nephew George inherited.

Edward Chetham died in 1769, his eldest sister Alice Bland a widow, inherited, and in 1774 Turton Tower passed to her only daughter Mary, who was married to Mordecai Green, a Spanish merchant.

Later, in 1835, James Green's eldest daughter Mary Anne sold it to James Kay, of Pendleton, a cotton spinner, who resided there restoring the building to its former condition.

Turton Tower remained the property of the Kay family until 1890, then was sold to the Appletons who let it to tenants.

In 1903, Sir Lees Knowles, Bart, C.V.O., purchased it, then in 1930, the Lady Nina Knowles presented the Tower with eight acres of parkland and three cottages to Turton Urban District Council, in memory of her husband. They were formally handed over in 1934, and opened as a Museum.

In the Entrance Hall is an example of one of the last types of armour worn in England and early seventeenth century. This is from the Bradshaw Hall collection.

The Dining Room, (now used by the Council as a committee room), is the oldest part of Turton Tower and was built about the twelfth century. In the south wall is the large mullioned window which was added in the late sixteenth century by the Orrells, its depth being increased in 1844. Some Swiss painted glass can be seen at the top.

There is a carved oak refectory table, and an iron-bound box which bears the inscription 'Humphrey Chetham Esquire's Charity 1748'. He was a descendant of the former Humphrey.

The Drawing Room (now used as the Council Chamber), has some fine pewter plate which came from Bradshaw Hall, and a grandfather clock thought to have been made by Samuel Crompton.

The Ashworth Room was named after Alderman G. H. Ashworth M.A., J.P., who helped to found the Turton Museum. Most of the furniture in this room came from Bradshaw Hall which was partly demolished in 1948. As well as items of local interest this contains brass, paintings, a carved oak court cabinet showing early English inlaid work, and an interesting crib dating 1667.

Moving to the Bradshaw Room, one finds a remarkable carved oak tester bed with its 'tester' or canopy, above. Also here is a carved oak cradle dated 1630. The story goes that a Royalist hid at Bradshaw Hall during which time he betrayed one of the daughters of the House. The girl's brother fought a duel with him while she watched through a window, rocking the cradle at the same time. The cradle (said to have been very unlucky) still rocks.

Not far from the Tower was a small farmhouse known as Timberbottom or 'The Skull House'. Unfortunately this is no longer in existence. In its possession were two skulls (male and female) which had been discovered in Bradshaw Brook in 1750. One of them appeared to have been pierced by a blow from a sharp instrument. It was said that if the skulls were not kept in the house, or if separated, the inmates would be constantly disturbed. They were placed on the mantelpiece at Timberbottom Farm. Many disturb-

WARDLEY HALL. Front and Rear. Photographs by Terry Husband.

ances followed, footsteps, sounded to be going to an upper room where in ghostly light two men appeared to be fighting while a ghostly figure of a girl watched. The farmer had the two skulls buried in Bradshaw Churchyard about 1840, but the weird happenings continued. So the skulls were dug up and placed on the family Bible in the study at Bradshaw Hall. These skulls remain together on the Bradshaw Hall family Bible to this day in a showcase in the Turton Tower Museum, and as long as they are left to rest here seem quite content, and in perfect harmony. They have chosen a Good and Wonderful place.

WARDLEY HALL

SITUATED in Worsley, about six miles from Manchester, on the site of a still older House, in a small woody Lancashire glade, and built, it is said by Thurstan Tyldesley during the reign of Edward VI; the picturesque black-and-white half-timbered structure of Wardley Hall which is at the time of writing this book, the official residence of the Bishop of Salford, is of quadrangular form, its covered archway opening into a courtyard in the centre, which measures about fifty feet by thirty-five feet. The Great Hall dates back to the Perpendicular Period.

Scores of lovely trees have sadly been demolished to make way for the North-easterly extension of the M62 Lancashire-Yorkshire motorway from Worsley. Long ago, Wardley Hall was almost completely surrounded by a moat; entrance being effected over a drawbridge through a gatehouse.

The Tyldesleys became Lords of Wardley by marriage with the Worsleys in the reign of Henry IV. The last Tyldesley was another Thurstan.

On the eve of the 'civil wars' the Hall became the residence of Roger Downes, of Wardley, whose son John married Penelope, daughter of Sir Cecil Trafford. They had a son Roger Downes, and a daughter, Penelope, who married Richard Savage, fourth Earl Rivers, a soldier and statesman—to whom she later conveyed the estate. He died about 1714 leaving a daughter Elizabeth, who was married to James, the fourth Earl of Barrymore who came from an Irish family. They also had an only daughter named Penelope, who became the wife of James, son of George, Earl of Cholmondeley who died in 1775.

A human skull is always kept on the top-stair of the staircase in a small aperture, and through exposure to the weather is bleached white. Legend once said it belonged to Roger Downes who was last male representative of the family. He was a dissolute person at the Court of Charles II. While in London, probably while in a drunken state, he threatened to kill the first man he met. The victim was a poor tailor through whom he ran his sword without mercy. Soon afterwards, goes the story, a watchman severed Downes' head from his body. The head was sent in a box to his sister who lived at Wardley Hall. Roger Downes died on the 27th June 1676, aged only twenty-eight.

Another later version tells us the skull belonged to fifty-five year old Edward Barlow, who was hanged-drawn-and-quartered in a most gruesome manner on September 10th 1641, at Lancaster for being a Priest, during the reign of William III. A relative of the family at Wardley, his head was taken there to be preserved as a relic of his martyrdom. It was said to have had red hair.

Edward Barlow of Barlow Hall was an executed Papist and later specified as Blessed Ambrose Barlow —Edward Barlow took the name Ambrose on joining the Benedictine Order.

A most precise scientific investigation of the skull was conducted in 1959-60 at St Bartholomew's Hospital, London and the report said that beyond any reasonable doubt the skull belonged to Blessed Ambrose Barlow.

Strangely enough the family vault of the Downes in Wigan Church was said to have been opened in 1779, and the skeleton of young Roger Downes was there complete with head.

There is positive evidence that the skull was impaled after death and not buried. A portrait which still exists was painted of Ambrose Barlow after death, and this was proved by Professor Cave at St Bartholomew's to represent the same person to whom the skull belonged. Its owner seems to have been—and still *is* very much attached to Wardley Hall for it is said to have gone through fire and water to remain there. Many old wives tales were told which have improved through the years. A maid was reported to have discovered the skull in the house, and thinking it had belonged to an animal threw it into the moat. Terrible storms arose causing much damage, but when the moat was drained and the skull returned to the Hall peace reigned once more.

So the fact remains that Roger Downes did *not* lose his head except for the very top of the crown, which had no doubt been removed to discover the cause of death. So the skull of Wardley Hall is treated with the respect it demands, for whenever moved it returns to its former resting-place, perhaps seeking refuge in the House it loved—who knows?

WORSLEY OLD HALL

WORSLEY HALL is said to date from the time of the Conquest 1066, when the owner was an eminent hero Eliseus de Workesley or (Worsley) one of the first Norman Barons who joined in the first crusade. His personal friend Robert, Duke of Normandy persuaded Worsley to accompany him in trying to rescue the Holy Land from the Saracens. It was for this that Robert relinquished his claims to the English Crown and mortgaged the revenues of his Norman duchy.

Elias or (Eliseus) de Worsley met many enemies it is said in the form of giants, saracens, and dragons, and is believed to have conquered and slain them all.* On arriving at Rhodes he emulated More of More Hall by encountering a venomous serpent which was causing devastation in the district. Unfortunately he failed in this combat and died. He was buried on the spot. Elias was so strong and brave he became known as a *giant* named Elias Gigas. Fighting many battles for religion and achieving outstanding victories which gave rise to the legend. The serpent probably being chosen to typify the crafty dealings by which a certain landowner tried to get rich at the expense of others.

Elias Gigas's descendants were owners of Worsley until the end of Edward IIIs reign when the line of

* Sir William de la More, of More Hall, in 1326 was a noted warrior and distinguished himself in the battle of Poictiers. Was knighted by Edward I and legend says became a hero by slaying 'The Dragon of Wantley' which was said to have seven heads and fourteen eyes.

WARDLEY HALL, COURTYARD.

WARDLEY HALL. Staircase showing
small aperture with skull.

male heirs ended, and by the marriage of its heiress came into the possession of Sir John Massey of Tatton, Cheshire. The Massey line ended after three generations and Tatton in Cheshire together with Worsley, went to William Stanley Esq., of Tatton and Worsley through marriage. The estates then passed to the Breretons of Malpas, Cheshire.

The present Hall is thought to have been built around 1550, the owner at that time being the last Brereton, Sir Richard, who married Dorothy Egerton of Ridley in 1572. Sir Richard died in 1598 without issue, and Lady Dorothy married Sir Peter Legh, of (Lyme) Stockport.

The ghost of Sir Richard caused consternation in Worsley village. Seven Priests tried to exorcise it, sacrificing a cock. This was futile as Sir Richard still made his presence conspicuous. After further entreaties from priests Sir Richard agreed to cut his visits down to once a year, and then take the form of a swallow. So he spread his tiny ectoplasm wings and probably still returns to the nest.

Sir Richard Brereton's estate passed to Dame Dorothy's half-brother, Sir Thomas Egerton, Lord Chancellor of England during the reign of James I. He became first Baron Ellesmere in 1602. About 1617 he was created Viscount Brackley, the courtesy-title borne by the eldest sons of the Earls of Ellesmere.

Lady Ellesmere fell downstairs and was killed—her ghost is also said to haunt the premises. Hers is possibly the one kindred spirit who welcomes the return of the ghostly swallow.

(It was a much later descendant Lord Brackley, son of a later Lord Ellesmere who on his return from the South African War was honoured by a large bonfire in Worsley, which burnt for three days. This was comprised of about six canal barges, railway sleepers, pit props etc.)

John, the second Viscount Brackley, son of the first, was created Earl of Bridgewater. In 1630 he bought out Lady Dorothy's life interest in the estate, but mostly lived at the family seat of Ashridge, Hertfordshire.

Father and son married mother and daughter. The Earl of Bridgewater's wife was Lady Frances Stanley, daughter of Lord Chancellor Ellesmere's third wife, the Countess Dowager of Derby, widow of Ferdinando, the fifth Earl.

In 1631, the Earl of Bridgewater was appointed Lord President of Wales. The estates passed to his son John the second Earl of Bridgewater, who was a friend of Milton the poet. Like his father *his* son another John succeeded, he became first Lord-Commissioner of the Admiralty.

The fourth Earl was Scroop, who in 1720 was created Duke of Bridgewater. His wife was a daughter of the Duke of Marlborough. He was succeeded by his son John second Duke of Bridgewater who died in 1748.

His younger brother Francis the third Duke of Bridgewater (the seventh child) and builder of the canals followed. He was born on 21st May 1736. Francis was sent abroad by his guardians the Duke of Bedford and Lord Trentham (afterwards Earl Gower and Marquis of Stafford) who'd married the young Duke's sister.

As far back as 1737 an act was passed by parliament to make Worsley Brook navigable to its junction, at the instance of the first Duke.

In 1759 Francis, Duke of Bridgewater when aged twenty-three, settled at Worsley old Hall, and in the same year made his first application to Parliament for a canal act which would enable him to construct a canal from Worsley to Salford, primarily to extend the Manchester market for coal.

Now James Brindley, a Derbyshire craftsman's son comes into the picture. Born in 1716, three miles north-east of Buxton, Brindley was twenty years the Dukes senior. He started by making models of mills, and took great delight in watching water-wheels and cog-wheels working, afterwards copying them in pieces of wood. He had no technical education. At the age of thirteen he became a millwright's apprentice to Abraham Bennet at Gurnett, Nr Macclesfield, and after serving his time started at Leek, showing remarkable skill. He chopped down his own timber to use. Brindley rapidly made fame.

About a year before the Duke arrived at Worsley, Brindley was busy on a survey made under Lord Gower's auspices for the canal between the two rivers Mersey and Trent. He could barely read and write, his worst subject was spelling, yet the Duke of Bridgewater decided he was the right man for him. And so in 1759, Brindley, the Duke, and John Gilbert, busily planned for the canal to pass over the river on a stone aqueduct while at Worsley Hall. On commencing, Brindley showed much ingenuity, from tunnelling the hill near Worsley to connect the canal with the Duke's coal-workings, applying a clay puddle to prevent the water soaking through the embankments, and inventing a new line for the extensive masonry required. He constructed a crane to lift the coal through a shaft at Manchester. And on the 17th July 1761, the first boat-load of coal was slowly bourne along Barton Aqueduct—one of the wonders of England. The cost for the construction of the canal was about £1,000 a mile. While employed by the Duke, Brindley's wages were one guinea a week. There being a shortage of money, many a committee of 'Ways and Means' was held by the Duke, Gilbert, and Brindley, at a small public house on the moss 1½ miles from Worsley, over their pipes and ale. The amount expended on all canals operations was £220,000. The annual revenue from the canals reached £80,000.

The locks were opened in 1772, and 'THE HEART OF OAK' a vessel of fifty tons passed through on its journey to Liverpool. The main part of the Duke's canal-making was finished when he was only aged thirty-six, but there was much developing to do afterwards, and he spent nearly £170,000 in making subterranean tunnels, the underground canals extended to forty miles long. The tonnage carried on the canal by 1845 had reached 480,626 tons. The Manchester Ship Canal was opened in 1894.

The Duke had a brick Hall built while the old building became a farm and living-quarters for canal workers. Another new Hall had been built by 1837, and the brick one demolished to make way for Leigh Road. The New Hall was also demolished in 1946. A case of the old surviving the new, and even the old Hall has been considerably altered, but still has some of the original plaster panelling, and now has sixty-three rooms.

The Duke in his later years was a heavily built man with features rather like those of George III, and wore a brown suit with dark breeches fastening at the knee with silver buckles. He owned one of the finest picture galleries in Europe. Having been disappointed in women with two broken engagements, first to Miss Jane Revell, and second Elizabeth, Duchess of Hamilton, he would only employ men-servants, by whom he

WORSLEY OLD HALL.

Painting, Margaret Chapman.

was respected as a good and just master, though stern and precise. These Ladies preferred to seek a more wealthy partner.

This great and famous Duke of Bridgewater died on the 8th March 1803, after a short illness caused through a chill, and was buried in the family vault at Ashridge his seat in Hertfordshire. Francis, was the sixth Earl, the third, last, and only bachelor Duke of Bridgewater. The Earldom passed to his cousin General Edward Egerton, then on to the eighth Earl, who died in Paris in 1829. The Duke of Bridgewater bequeathed his canal-property devolved under trust to Lord Francis Leveson Gower and Lord Francis Egerton, afterwards first Earl of Ellesmere. The Bridgewater Trust is now a thing of the past, but the famous canals remain as a great achievement.

Worsley Old Hall remained a private House until about 1940, when it was taken over by the National Coal Board as offices. They moved out in March 1965, and the south-east Lancashire and north-east Cheshire Traffic Committee moved in, but they also moved out in 1966, so time marches on. There was once a Roman road running through the grounds but no trace of this can be found today, but several underground tunnels are said to run from the Hall, one to Worsley Church.

In 1968, great activity was aroused in Lancashire with the 'Operation Springclean' campaign. Buildings, statues, etc., being scrubbed and years of industrial grime removed. Parks and gardens re-planned; houses painted in bright colours, making the County worthy of our Lancastrian pride, and fit for the visit of Her Majesty Queen Elizabeth II who in the 'Merry month of May' during her journey through Lancashire, made it a memorable occasion for amongst other places, Worsley, where she stood on the famous hump-backed bridge over the Bridgewater Canal to view the canal basin. Her Majesty also saw a small exhibition arranged by local historian Mr Frank Mullineux, consisting of pictures showing something of the history of Worsley, and was delighted to see an old picture of Queen Victoria her great-great-grandmother who visited the town in 1851.

This was the first visit of a Royal Sovereign for almost thirty years, the last time being during the 1940s, when their Majesties King George VI and Queen Elizabeth the Queen Mother, went to see the Walkden High Level Station. Unfortunately owing to war restrictions this was a quiet secret occasion.

The owners of Worsley Hall are the Bridgewater Estates Limited, but the fate of this interesting Hall is uncertain. The District Council have considered turning it into a Museum but expenses are too great. Surely this most important link with our British History is worth preserving.

WYECOLLER HALL

WYECOLLER HALL, Near Colne, was the seat of the Cunliffe's of Billington for many years. Names of successive members of the family are attached to documents relating to the property of the Abbots of Whalley. Difficulties prevailed and their ancestral estates passed into other hands.

In the days of the commonwealth their loyalty cost them dear, and the family eventually settled at Wyecoller. The last of the line died about 1819, and the Hall became a mass of ruins.

In the following legend tradition says that a ghostly horseman visits Wyecoller once a year, dressed in the costume of the Stuart Period. Strange that on these evenings the weather is always wild and tempestuous with no moonlight. When the wind is at its height the horseman is heard dashing up the road at full speed, he crosses a narrow bridge and stops at the Hall door, dismounts, and makes his way up some stairs into one of the rooms of the house. A woman's dreadful screams are heard, and groans. The horseman appears at the door; mounts his steed and gallops off. The horse seems wild with rage with fire streaming from its nostrils. Tradition says a member of the Cunliffe family murdered his wife in that room, and that the ghostly horseman was the murderer, who is doomed to pay this annual visit to the home of his victim.

ACKNOWLEDGEMENTS

The author extends her sincere thanks to the following for their kind assistance, and permission to include their Houses.

The Right Hon. The Earl of Derby, M.C. (Knowsley Hall).

Sir H. P. Anthony M. de Hoghton, Bart. (Hoghton Tower).

Richard Cavendish Esq., (Holker Hall).

Colonel Robert G. Parker, D.S.O., F.S.A., J.P. (Browsholme Hall).

Major James R. Reynolds (Leighton Hall).

Mr Wilfred Heap (Extwistle Hall), Robert Kirkham, Mr I. J. Thompson, with special thanks to Geoffrey Stott, for untiring assistance in research for Extwistle Hall, and several other Houses.

Mr Kenneth Fielding, and Miss Patience Anne Aspinall (Hurstwood Hall).

Eric F. Lavery Esq., (Osbaldeston Hall), and Miss Pamela Lavery.

The owners of Barcroft Hall, and other additional Houses mentioned.

Manchester City Art Galleries.

The Local History Library, Manchester Public Libraries.

Chetham's Hospital and Library, Manchester, and Mr H. Vickers, House Governor.

Mr Gerald B. Cotton, F.L.A., Senior Lecturer of Manchester College of Commerce.

City of Salford Art Galleries and Museums, and Stanley Shaw, F.R.E.S., A.M.A. Director.

City of Liverpool Art Galleries and Museums, and Stanley Holmes, Town Clerk of Speke Corporation.

Bolton Corporation Museum and Art Gallery, and Mr V. C. Smith, F.M.A., F.G.S. Director.

The Corporation of Chorley and John Binns, L.Inst., P.A., M.Inst., B.C.A. Superintendent.

County Borough of Burnley Art Gallery and Museum, and Mr H. G. Thornton, Curator.

County Borough of Wigan, and John Ashton, F.Inst., P.R.A. (DIP) M.Inst., B.C.A. Director.

Mr. H. H. G. Arthur, F.L.A., F.R.S.A. Borough Librarian and Curator, Central Library, Wigan.

The Chadderton Urban District Council, and P. W. Musther, F.C.I.S. Solicitor and Clerk of the Council.

The Borough of Leigh, and James Blackburn, F.L.A. Borough Librarian.

Reginald Dart, C.Eng., M.I., Mun.E., Dist., T.P., A.M.T.P.I. Hon. Curator of The Turton Tower Museum.

The Gawthorpe Foundation, and Commander James Pearson, R.N. Organizing secretary.

WORSLEY OLD HALL.

Her Majesty Queen Elizabeth II on humped-backed
bridge over Bridgewater Canal, Worsley.

The National Trust, and Rufford Old Hall Management Committee, and George C. Miller, Hon. Curator.

The Samlesbury Hall Guide Book by George Eastwood, published by the Samlesbury Hall Trust, John B. Jackson, M.H.C.I. Manager, and Geoffrey R. Cunliffe, Assistant Secretary.

Major Nicholas Bacon, M.A. (Cam).

The Reverend John Allen, (Wardley Hall).

Mr R. Sharpe France, M.A. County Archivist, Preston.

Mr Harry W. Charlton, Manager, Swinton & Pendlebury Journal.

Victor Zorian, Editor, 'Lancashire Life'.

Tom Bergin, Editor, 'Salford City Reporter'.

Swinton and Pendlebury Public Libraries, M. W. Devereux, F.L.A., Borough Librarian, and Diana Winterbotham, Reference and Local History Librarian; The Stretford Central Library, and Miss F. Scattergood, F.L.A.

MANCHESTER PUBLIC LIBRARY

Most of the photographs reproduced in this book have been supplied by them. We wish to thank them for their valuable assistance.